As published in the

TOMBSTONE TIMES

Tombstone Arizona's History & Information Journal

TOMBSTONE

STORIES

1879 - 1883

BY KATHY FRANZ

LifeHouse
Publishing
Littleton, CO

TABLE OF CONTENTS

INTRODUCTION

Tombstone in its early years, 1879 through 1883, is filled with great stories of men, women, critters and mines. Of course, there were a lot of gamblers, rustlers, and criminals of all kinds, too.

Ed Schieffelin discovered silver in 1877 and people by the thousands flocked to the area and started building small towns. Tombstone became the largest, and life in Tombstone was rough. Mining the silver was hard work and selling goods and services to the miners happened round-the-clock.

Some recreation was needed, so along came the saloons, theatres and dancing halls. Music was plentiful from local citizens and traveling musicians, and even the circus came to town.

Tombstone enjoyed celebrating holidays from parades on New Year's Day to parties at Christmas. A Valentine's Day-type love could be found and, unfortunately, some were even killed for love.

With every Western town came stories of items lost, found, stolen or strayed. All sorts of animal stories abounded, from kettled dogs to displayed gila monsters to wrestling brown bears.

All the below stories were originally published as articles in *the Tombstone Times* from July 2019 through April 2022. Owners and editors Keith Davis and Janice Hendricks were the first to have faith in my articles and publish them. This book is dedicated to them.

COWBOYS, GOOD AND BAD

Cowboys, published April 2021

On October 5, 1881, an unsigned article appeared on page 1 of the Tombstone Nugget newspaper. The writer is well-educated and has a good command of grammar and the English language, especially adjectives.

A Description of the Manners and Customs of the Native.

"Having spent a goodly portion of my days as a cow boy, I consider myself practically qualified to write on the subject. The boyhood sport of the cow boy is not with marbles or balls or tops, but with a lariat or rope of rawhide, with which he lassoes calves and everything, animate or inanimate, over which a loop can be thrown. At seven years of age he is an expert horseman, and able to do service on the range in many ways. Between this age and manhood he acquires some knowledge of the "three R's" though seldom at school, and at sixteen is usually as good a horseman and as dexterous a roper as any man in the district.

He is never fleshy or large-limbed, is slightly bow-legged from constant riding, is endowed with more than average muscular strength, and is very active and capable of great endurance. He is an unerring shot, and cool in time of danger. He smokes cigarittes [sic], chews tobacco, drinks whisky, carries a six shooter, and is guilty of many vices that would, if enumerated, shock the embezzeler and stock gambler of civilized regions. He is not more quarrelsome than man in general but, unfortunately, his quarrels are apt to result in homicide.

The property of the cow boy is a wiry pony, a saddle and a lariat. The pony or "plug" is of Spanish stock, active and enduring. It is a stranger to the touch of currycomb and brush, and don't know corn from beans. The saddle is a ponderous affair of wood and leather, weighing from ten to fifteen pounds. It has a pommel varying in diameter from three to six inches. Costly saddles sometimes have silver stars plentifully besprinkled on available parts of their surface. Two girths or sinches are necessary to hold the saddle firmly in position – a forward and a flank girth. The lariat is about forty feet long, and is composed of eight pliable rawhide thongs plaited into a rope about half an inch in diameter. At one end is a ring; and at the other a loop to fit over the saddle pommel.

The wardrobe of the cow boy is unique. He wears a broad-brimmed straw or wool hat. His jacket is of ducking, his shirt of calico or hickory, and his pantaloons of some stout stuff over which are worn leather leggings. Heavy boots with high heels, to which are attached a pair of spurs with two inch rowels, complete his outfit. When the weather is threatening, he straps behind his saddle a slicker of oiled linen, which reaches from head to heels.

Thus accoutered, the cow boy is ready for business. He is employed either to drive a herd to Kansas or to look after those on the range. The spring is his harvest time. Then the great herds are put up for the drive. This is the season, too, when the annual round-up occurs, for the purpose of apportioning the unmarked calves and yearlings among the owners of stock on the range, that they may be branded with the particular device adopted by each as his distinguishing mark, generally the initial of his name. The law requires the brand to be recorded in the County Clerk's office, together with ear marks, crops, half crops, upper and under bits, upper and under slopes, splits, swallow-forks, and jinglebobs. [A swallow-fork is made by a triangular cut of the calf's ear, and jinglebobs are made by slashing the ear in half letting the two halves dangle near the head.]

The cow boy's life is not an easy one. During the whole year he is in the saddle from daylight until dark. His diet is bread, bacon and coffee. When on the trail, in addition to driving during the day, he is compelled to guard the cattle during a part of the night, the force being divided into three reliefs for this purpose. In case of a stampede he must ride night and day. In spite of all this, the cow boy is healthy and cheerful. No one is more hospitable, and his bravery is proverbial. But he is a relic of barbarism and must go, and the places that have known him will not mourn his departure, for he is too much addicted to "whooping 'em up."

Zwing Hunt, published February 2022

This is a true story of two descendants of Jesse and Lucy. One descendant became an outlaw and was killed by Apaches, like his step-brother, and the other one became President of the United States.

Texas Beginnings

Zwing Hunt was born on March 29, 1858, probably in Burnet County, Texas, northwest of Austin. His mother Mary Ann Elizabeth (nee Johnson) married widower Thomas W. Hunt who had three children by his first marriage. In 1860, Thomas was a stockraiser, and the children were Mary, age 10, Joel, age 4, and Zwingle, age 2.

Kopperl Street Scene-1880's

from Bosque County: Land and People, p 59.

The family moved north, and in 1880, they were in Kopperl, Bosque County, southwest of Fort Worth. Zwing's father was a miller, his brother Hugh was 19 and a stockraiser, Lucy 16, sister Frankie 14, Sam 10, and sister Tommie 8. However, Zwing was not listed with them.

The mill was bought from Green Powell and was located in "Powell Dale" at the connection of the Mesquite Creek with the Brazos River, south of Kopperl. "A dam or dike was built on the creek to store water to channel down a rock-lined ditch past a mill wheel and back into the creek. The mill took in wheat and corn and milled it into flour and meal."

Thomas also had a store in Kopperl and was a trustee at Community School #12. Hugh was Powell Dale's postmaster.

Arizona Territory

Zwing's half-brother Joel Ponton Hunt had been in the Arizona Territory for several years. He had a freight company that hauled between Tombstone and New Mexico. In March 1879, he decided to start prospecting at the base of Star Peak, west of Hillsboro, New Mexico.

Dr. Warren of Hillsboro told the Mesilla Valley newspaper that Joel was an industrious, enterprising miner. He was cutting timber the first week of June, probably on the 3rd, when he was attacked by Apaches. He was driving a six-mule team and was instantly killed by a shot through the right lung. The team took fright breaking the wagon into pieces. Five of his mules were later found.

The 9th Cavalry had encountered Victorio's band in a canyon in the Mimbres Mountains just four days earlier. When negotiations broke down, the Apaches fled on foot without leaving a trail. The Cavalry destroyed the Apache camp, so it was surmised that Joel was killed by Victorio's roaming band near the head of the Mimbres.

Victorio

3

Zwing was sent to the Arizona Territory to get Joel's freighting equipment. He decided to stay in the area and became associated with Billy Grounds. Zwing worked for the Chiricahua Cattle Company, and the company loaned him money to freight lumber from Morse's sawmill to Tombstone. The two stole horses from his previous company, and on October 13, 1881, they stole 30 head of cattle from James C. Persley/Pursley and Mr. Woolfe at Sulphur Springs. The cattle were found in Contention, and a larceny warrant for stealing the cattle was issued for the two.

Zwing was also known as "Curly's boy." Curly Bill Brocius was a well-known outlaw in the Arizona Territory. He was suspected of cattle rustling and stayed in the town of Galeyville quite often.

According to the *Tombstone Epitaph,* Zwing was "tall and slim, quite sandy complexioned, sandy mustache, and his face, neck, and hands badly freckled." In the 1882 census, Zwing was living in Pine Cañon, Arizona, near Camp Bowie. This is now on route 42 west of Galeyville.

A Robbery Gone Bad

Zwing and Billy Grounds allegedly attempted to rob the Tombstone Mining and Milling office at 8:20 p.m. on the night of March 25, 1882. Superintendent W. L. Austin, George Cheney, and company assayer Mr. F. F. Hunt were there with civil engineer Martin Peel.

Martin was a 26-year-old civil engineer employed by the local mills in the rebuilding of the dam and repair of the flume. He spent his evenings socially in the office with other workers, and this evening, he was sitting closest to the door.

When the door burst opened, Billy and Zwing leveled their Winchester rifles at the men. Mr. Austin was reaching for his gun as well as Martin. In the next instant, Martin was shot in the heart, and the other three men ducked behind a counter.

Startled and without getting any money, Zwing and Billy fled. One lost his white hat outside. It was later identified as Zwing's and had been previously owned by Fin Clanton and T. J. Harrison. Governor Frederick Augustus Tritle offered a $500 reward for the arrest of the murderers; however, the coroner's jury decided Martin's death was by unknown parties.

Four days later, Zwing and Billy were at Chandler's Ranch saying the owner owed them money. John Elliott and a Mr. Caldwell were there, too. A man was sent to Tombstone to get the money, but instead, he told the sheriff about Zwing and Billy.

Deputies William "Billy" M. Breakenridge, Tombstone jailer E. H. Allen, John Gillespie, and Allen "Jack" Young went to arrest the two. At 6 a.m., a pack of dogs barked their arrival, so one of them rapped on the door. The lawmen were told the two were not there and to go to the lower house. However, the lawmen returned – Breakenridge to the front door, Allen on the south side, and Young and Gillespie to the rear door.

Billy Breakenridge

The rear door opened, and Deputy John Gillespie was immediately shot dead through the left breast and left temple. Jack Young was shot through the front of his thigh about 6" below the waistband.

A teamster staying overnight named A. "Bull" Lewis came out the front door, and someone behind him started firing. Deputy Allen was creased in the right neck and was dragged behind a dry creek bank. Breakenridge and Lewis hid behind oak trees. Breakenridge fired through the open door and hit Billy Grounds. Zwing came around the house and was shot by Breakenridge and Allen. Breakenridge got a minor wound on his right hand.

Billy Grounds got buckshot in the head and face, two on the right side of the neck, one in the right breast, and one in the left shoulder. He never regained consciousness and died the next day at the Tombstone hospital. George Whitwell Parsons called Grounds "Curly Bill's Kid," and suggested it was "either robbery or thirst for gore against the Tombstone Mine Company's attitude toward the cowboys." The *Nugget* newspaper said Grounds was buried nude in Boothill.

According to the *Tombstone Epitaph,* Billy was "quite a young man, with a round, red face, and of shorter stature than … Hunt." Author Grace McCool wrote that Billy was 20 years old, his real name was Boucher, and he came from a respectable family. Dr. Goodfellow found buckshot partly embedded in several thick folds of a silk handkerchief worn around Billy's neck when he was shot. This was the second time Dr. Goodfellow found a bullet that did not pass through a silk handkerchief.

Zwing was shot through the left lung, and per Breakenridge, "every breath he drew whistled out through the wound in his back."

Zwing's Escape

Zwing was brought to the Tombstone hospital and left unguarded because "he could not turn himself over in bed, much less walk, or even stand upon his feet." Dr. George Goodfellow and Supervisor Joyce felt it was too inhumane to remove him to jail and that he posed no chance of escape.

Zwing's brother Hugh came to Tombstone on April 16, and on April 27 between 8 and 9 p.m., Hugh helped Zwing escape from the front room of the hospital. Others in the back of the hospital heard nothing.

After going to the Dragoons to rest, they wandered in the Chiricahua mountains and the Swisshelms. Zwing told Hugh of a treasure buried in the Chiricahuas. On May 30, they left Sweetwater in the Swisshelms and went to Russels (Rustlers) Canyon on their way to Morse's Mill in Pinery Canyon. (Per author McCool, Rustlers Canyon was a favorite campsite of the Apaches, just four miles from Galeyville.)

The next morning, Apaches shot Zwing to death; he was hit in the left hip and abdomen with two in the head. Hugh ran from the Indians, mounted his hobbled horse, and went through the timber to Camp Price. Soldiers returned with him to the site and found Zwing dead with the middle finger of his right hand cut off. Zwing was buried there, and later William Breakenridge and Phil Montague from Tombstone exhumed the body and identified it for their records. As both Zwing and Billy Grounds were near penniless, Hugh requested only Zwing's horse and guns.

Hugh said that Zwing told him that he only shot at Chandler's Ranch because he thought it was the Earps. Morgan Earp had been shot and killed on March 18, and Wyatt Earp and his men were on their Vendetta Ride looking for Morgan's killers.

Epilogue

In 1900, Zwing's brother Hugh was married with four children and was a traveling salesman living in Oak Cliff, a suburb of Dallas. In 1910, he was in machinery sales, and he died in 1914. He is buried in the Kopperl Cemetery near his parents. The Powell Dale area became mostly buried with the building of the Whitney Dam in 1951. A part of the old mill race may still be seen when the lake level is low.

And for the President? You may have guessed it as Zwing's mother was a Johnson. Her brother Samuel Ealy Johnson, Sr., was the grandfather of our 36th President, Lyndon Baines Johnson, born August 27, 1908.

Oh, and the buried treasure in the Chiricahuas? It was never found.

Note: This story was also published in my book *We Sent 'Em to Boothill.*

THE EARP BROTHERS

"Always Virge and Morg" or "Why Wasn't Wyatt Shot?"

published May 2021

Wyatt Earp has the reputation of never being shot – well, except once. While leaning back in a chair, his single-action revolver fell out of his holster with the bullet going through his coat and ending up in the ceiling. With his years in Tombstone and all its mayhem, why was Wyatt never shot? Did he secretly belong to an opposing gang? Was he buddy-buddy with everyone who drank and gambled at the Oriental saloon? Or was everyone afraid of retribution from his friend Doc Holliday? Let's take a look at the Earp brothers and their enemies.

Wyatt

 Wyatt arrived in Tombstone on December 1, 1879, with plans to run a stage coach line. Two already existed, so he and his brothers found other employment. Wyatt went into gambling as did his brother James. Wyatt later received ¼ interest in the Oriental saloon for his services as manager and enforcer. He also ran a faro game at the Eagle Brewery and owned a race horse named "Sorrel Reuben." Brother Virgil owned the race horse named "Old Doc." Wyatt met Fred Dodge, undercover agent for Wells, Fargo & Co., and was appointed stagecoach messenger (i.e. shotgun rider.) Wyatt also was into mining; he filed documents for the Northern Extension Mountain Maid Mine with some of his brothers and R. J. Winders. From July 27 to November 9, 1880, Wyatt was deputy sheriff under Charles Shibell.

Virgil's wife Allie purportedly said in *Tombstone Travesty* that Wyatt "was always kneadin' his knuckles and shufflin' cards to keep his hands in shape for gamblin.' . . . But mostly he was out sizin' up the town." Per George Whitwell Parson's diary on October 27, the day after the O. K. Corral shoot-out: "Desperate men and a desperate encounter. Bad blood has been brewing some time and I was not surprised at the outbreak. . . . It has been a bad scare and the worst is not yet over some think." Fred Dodge said Wyatt continued about his business, "coming and going as usual and by his appearance no one would think that he had been through an ordeal like the one just passed." After Virgil was shot on December 28, 1881, Wyatt was appointed U.S. Deputy Marshall taking Virgil's place. Deputy Sheriff William Breakenridge wrote in his book *Helldorado* that Wyatt never went out without a bodyguard of five to eight men whom he called his posse.

Wyatt and his enemies

#1. Ike Clanton. Ike said Wyatt offered him a bribe in June 1881 to lure the Billy Leonard gang to a place where they could be arrested or killed; thus, preserving his friend Doc Holliday from being accused of the Benson stagecoach robbery on March 15, 1881. Ike later testified that he jumped Leonard's ranch after the robbery and was later confronted by Leonard about it. On October 26, 1881, Ike was arrested for carrying arms and had words with Wyatt at the courthouse. Wyatt faced him at the O.K. Corral that afternoon but allowed Ike to run away as he was unarmed. In his testimony, Ike said earlier that day Wyatt said he would not fight "as there was no money in it." In February 1882, Ike charged Wyatt and others again with murder at the O.K. Corral, but the charge was again dismissed.

#2. Billy Clanton. Ike's brother Billy stole one of Wyatt's prize horses in December 1879. Wyatt did get the horse back about a year later, and Billy asked him if he had any more horses to lose.

#3. Frank McLaury. In late July 1880, Wyatt assisted his brother Virgil and the U.S. Army in locating six mules which were being rebranded at the McLaury Ranch. Wyatt said Frank warned him to never follow him again. A month later, Earp ran into Frank and brother Tom in Charleston, and they told him that they would kill him if he ever followed them as he had done before. In June 1881, Wyatt said he offered the same bribe to Frank as he had offered to Ike.

#4. Tom McLaury. Wyatt buffaloed Tom in the street shortly before the O.K. Corral shoot-out. Virgil's wife Allie said that James Earp's step-daughter Hattie was perhaps dating one of the McLaury's, and all the Earps were extremely angry at her. Per John Plesant Gray, even his father "told us early in the day that trouble was brewing between the Earps and McLowerys [sic], advising us to keep off the street ..." (Note: McLowerys, not Clantons.)

#5. Pete Spence. According to Allie, all the Earp wives were warned to stay away from Pete Spence's family who lived across the street from them. Wyatt along with his brother Morgan, Mr. Marshall Williams, and Deputy Sheriff William Breakenridge arrested Pete for the September 8th

Bisbee stagecoach robbery. Pete was later arrested a second time on a U.S. mail charge associated with this robbery.

#6. Frank Stilwell. Wyatt arrested Frank twice for the same robbery as Pete Spence. After the first arrest in Benson, Frank rode next to Wyatt on the way to the Tombstone jail. He threatened to kill Wyatt and the others – Morgan, Marshall Williams, and William Breakenridge. Spence and Stilwell's bail was paid by Ike Clanton, William Allen and C. H. "Ham" Light. At the O.K. Corral trial, Ham testified that the barber told him that "there would be trouble between the Earps and the cowboys."

Virgil

On his move to Tombstone, Virgil was appointed a U. S. Deputy Marshall in Tucson. Allie said that he also did odd jobs in Tombstone.

Virgil served two weeks as assistant city marshal (October 28 to November 15, 1880) and later became Tombstone's Chief of Police (June 6 to October 29, 1881.) In early October 1881, Apaches stole 14 horses from the McLaury ranch and three miles further, stole 12 from Frink's ranch. George Whitwell Parsons with 20 armed men composed the volunteer posse. They chose County Sheriff John Behan as Captain and Virgil as First Lieutenant.

George wrote in his diary: "Also there was Arizona's most famous outlaw at the present time 'Curly Bill' with two followers. He killed one of our former Marshals, and to show how we do things in Arizona, I will say that our present Marshal [Virgil Earp] and said "C Bill" shook each other warmly by the hand and hobnobbed together some time." Virgil had arrested Curly Bill when he shot City Marshall Fred White a year earlier.

On December 14, 1881, the Benson stagecoach was robbed. Milt Joyce of the Oriental hinted that the Earps and Doc Holliday might be responsible. Virgil hit Milt in the face, and Milt said to the Earp party: "Your favorite method is to shoot a man in the back, but if you murder me, you will be compelled to shoot me in front." Allie said that Virgil did have a temper. Before coming to Tombstone, Virgil had "whirred" Ben Baker by the nose, beat up Frank Shultz with a Mr. Hanson, and chased and beaten a stagecoach driver five miles who had hit his horse while passing him.

On December 28, Virgil was shot in the back by unknown assailants. Per George's diary: "Tonight about 11:30 Doc G[oodfellow] had just left and

I thought couldn't have crossed the street – when four shots were fired in quick succession from very heavily charged guns . . . Cries of "There they go," "Head them off" were heard but the cowardly apathetic guardians of the peace were not inclined to risk themselves and the other brave men, all more or less armed, did nothing." Sherman McMasters saw Ike Clanton in Charleston that night, and when asked about the shooting, Ike said "he would have to go back and do the job over."

Ike and brother Phin turned themselves in as did Pete Spence. However, for lack of evidence, the trial was dismissed on February 3.

Virgil and his enemies

#1. Ike Clanton. Ike was slapped by Danny McCann on June 9, 1881, and Virgil stopped their fight. On October 25, Virgil played cards all night with Ike, Tom McLaury, Johnny Behan, and one other. Leaving to go home the morning of the 26th, Virgil refused to carry Ike's message to Doc Holliday that Ike will kill him on sight. Later that morning, Ike was armed on the street, and Virgil buffaloed him. That afternoon Virgil was shot in the leg at the O. K. Corral. Ike allegedly shot Virgil on December 28.

#2. Frank McLaury. Like Wyatt above, Virgil reported that Frank accosted him and said, "If you ever again follow us as close as you did, then you will have to fight anyway."

#3. Tom McLaury. Tom also played cards all night with Virgil and was killed in the O.K. Corral shoot-out.

#4. Pete Spence. Pete was arrested twice for the September 8th Bisbee stagecoach robbery. Pete allegedly shot Virgil on December 28.

#5. Frank Stilwell. Frank was arrested twice for the same robbery as Pete Spence. After the second arrest, Virgil took Frank to Tucson. Frank allegedly shot Virgil on December 28.

#6. Hank Swilling. Allegedly shot Virgil on December 28.

#7. Johnny Ringo. The same.

#8. Johnny Barnes. The same. Johnny was dying when he told Fred Dodge that Doc Holliday was there at the Benson robbery on March 15, 1881.

Morgan

Morgan assisted Virgil at times as a special appointed deputy, succeeded Wyatt as a Wells, Fargo & Co. messenger, and was a dealer at the Oriental saloon.

However, Morgan was mostly known as a gambler who visited the town of Benson often. On March 15, 1881, Morgan was a shotgun messenger on the Benson stagecoach run. One of Leonard's gang, Jim Crane later told John Plesant Gray that the robbery was planned by the Earps. Morgan gave the tip that about $20,000 was in the strongbox. The holdup would have met with no resistance, but Bob Paul stepped in as messenger, and the robbery was thwarted. However, Bud Philpot and Peter Roerig were killed. John wrote that when Crane was at the Gray Ranch near Cloverdale, New Mexico, Frank Buckskin Leslie arrived to arrest Crane but didn't.

Crane died with Old Man Clanton at the Guadalupe Canyon massacre on August 13. On August 9, 1881, Morgan was hired by Deputy Sheriff McComas of Benson to arrest two men, "Off Wheeler" Harlan and James "Bones" McCarty for shooting at an Indian. This made Morgan a deputy for Sheriff John Behan.

On March 19, 1882, Morgan was killed. Per George's diary: "Poor Morgan Earp was shot through by an unknown party . . . The second shot was fired apparently at Wyatt Earp . . . Murderers got away, of course, but it was and is quite evident who committed the deed. The man was Stilwell in all probability. For two cowardly, sneaking attempts at murder, this and the shots at Virgil E when I came nearly getting a dose, rank at the head . . . Bad times ahead now.

"March 20, 1882: Morg Earp's body sent to Colton yesterday . . . and tonight came news of Frank Stilwell's body being found riddled with bullets and buckshot.

"A quick vengeance, and a bad character sent to Hell, where he will be the chief attraction until a few more accompany him."

Morgan and his enemies

#1. Ike Clanton. After the Philpot murder, Morgan asked Ike repeatedly if he would take Wyatt's bribe to lure the Leonard gang. On the morning of October 26, 1881, when Virgil buffaloed Ike, Morgan took him to court. When Wyatt and Ike had words in the courtroom about shooting each other, Morgan offered Ike his weapons back when Deputy Sheriff

Campbell stopped them. Ike was fined $25, and Virgil took Ike's guns to the Grand Hotel as ordered by the court.

#2. Frank McLaury. When Spence and Stilwell were arrested for the second time, Frank told Morgan that he would never be arrested. He would kill the Earps. On October 26, Morgan was shot through the shoulders at the O.K. Corral, and Frank was killed.

#3. Pete Spence. Pete was arrested twice for the September 8th Bisbee stagecoach robbery. He allegedly shot Morgan on March 18, 1882.

#4. Frank Stilwell. When Spence and Stilwell were first arrested in Bisbee, Frank rode next to Morgan on the way to the Tombstone jail. He told Morgan that he would kill him and the others with him – Wyatt, Marshall Williams, and William Breakenridge. Frank allegedly shot Morgan on March 18, 1882. Frank was killed the next day in Tucson by the Earps.

#5. A German man. Allegedly shot Morgan on March 18, 1882.

#6. Indian Charley. The same.

#7. An Indian man. The same.

Conclusion

After the shooting of Morgan, Allie lamented, "Always Virge and Morg." For five months – since the O.K. Corral – no one shot at Wyatt or Doc. They were out in public except for when they were in jail during the O.K. Corral trial.

Doc was threatened by Johnny Ringo on January 17, 1882, but they were both arrested and fined.

Perhaps, the Epitaph had the best reason when it stated on February 13, 1882: "Besides cowboys, there is a class much larger in numbers of the 'good Lord and good deed' kind, who keep up a secret partnership with the robbers and profit by their lawlessness."

Yes, perhaps, Wyatt and brother James had to be nice to everyone to keep them coming back to their gambling tables. It's the way they made their living. Wyatt had almost as many enemies as did his brothers Virgil and Morgan, yet he wasn't shot.

I believe that Wyatt played both sides of the fence – being buddy-buddy with everyone in the gambling halls, yet standing up for the law when others asked him to. I think he had a way of placating his enemies to keep them coming back to drink and gamble. Plus, he let Ike run away from the O.K. Corral fight, so Ike owed him.

John Plesant Gray agreed that stock raisers had to be nice to rustlers, so their stock wouldn't get stolen. John said about the Gray Ranch:

"There were no two ways about it – either we had to be hospitable to all travelers alike or they would soon give a ranch the bad name of turning the hungry wayfarer away from its door – and that would be the beginning of the end … If you hoped to survive you had to be a good neighbor to all. Your livestock, and, in fact, all your possessions were at the mercy of any enemy. And because of these facts, we found it always a wise policy never to carry firearms when at the home ranch and to always request visitors to leave their pistols or rifles with their saddles."

Only once did one of the rustlers steal from John, and he told Billy Leonard, who was called the captain, and the cartridges were returned. John was at the McLaury boys' camp in Sulphur Springs Valley a short time before the O. K. Corral shoot-out. Hungry and tired, they gave him a good meal and a fresh horse for the last 25 miles to Tombstone. "These boys were plain, good-hearted, industrious fellows. They may have harbored passing rustlers at their ranch, but what rancher did not?" Interestingly, John's father Mike Gray along with Ike Clanton and 18-year-old William Lee Gaston were the "disinterested appraisers" for the two McLaury estates.

It seems that the assassins were always after Virgil and Morgan. Both men were shot at the O.K. Corral, and then later both were shot in their backs by assassins hiding in the dark. No one was ever convicted for any of these shootings.

Sadly, Watt did not have faith in Tombstone's justice system to find the assassins, and rather took his vengeance out at a Tucson railroad station and during the Vendetta Ride.

Epilogue

During Wyatt's Vendetta Ride, Hank Swilling was reportedly killed in Fronteras, Mexico, where he had been with Ike Clanton, Pony Diehl, and Johnny Ringo. Johnny Ringo died on July 13, 1882, from a single gunshot wound to the head. On June 28, 1882, George wrote: "Met the notorious Pete Spence with a villainous-looking gang between Lewis and Crystal Springs (driving some cattle.)" Pete later spent 18 months in the Arizona Territorial Prison for pistol-whipping a man to death. He then partnered with Phin Clanton on a goat ranch near Globe. In April 1887, Phin was arrested for cattle rustling, and brother Ike was killed near Springerville on June 1, 1887. Phin died in 1906, and Pete married his widow in 1910. Pete died in 1914.

WANTED

READERS

Who are interested in
Tombstone, Arizona
and the West!

TombstoneTimes.com

FOUR FAMOUS MEN

Four Famous Men in Tombstone, published November 2021

Since Tombstone was known for its saloons and gambling houses, I will make you a bet. I bet you didn't know all the following four famous men were in Tombstone in 1881 and 1882. Any takers?

Bat Masterson was in Tombstone for a short time in February and March 1881. He was friends with Wyatt Earp, Luke Short, and Charley Storms. He witnessed the killing of Storms by Short on February 25.

The *Daily Deadwood Pioneer Times* of March 13, 1881, reprinted the *Tombstone Daily Nugget's* article about the shooting. According to Short, Storms had been drinking heavily, playing cards and abusing him verbally. They had spoken outside, but Storms relented and went back inside to gamble. After Short got off duty at 1 p.m., he was outside with Bat and Storm's partner, Mr. "Dublin" Lyon. Storms pulled him into the street and pulled out his pistol. Short pulled his, and both shot simultaneously. Short twirled around to be sure Storm's partner was gone. Storms was on the ground moving his eyes, and Short shot him again.

Bat told his story in *Human Life* which was reprinted in the *Washington Post* on March 31, 1907. His story is a little different. "Charley was one of the best-known gamblers in the entire West, and had, on several occasions, successfully defended himself in pistol fights with Western gunfighters. Storms did not know Short and had sized him up as an insignificant looking fellow whom he could slap in the face without expecting a return." Both were about to pull their pistols, when Bat stopped the fight. He took Charley outside and then walked him home as he had been "up all night and had been quarreling with other persons." Storms returned, pulled Short off the sidewalk, and aimed his Colt cut-off .45 caliber, single action, at him. Short put his pistol against Storms' heart and shot. Short was exonerated.

Shortly thereafter, Bat left Tombstone for Dodge City and then Colorado. In April 1883 in an effort to curb vice in Dodge City, newly-elected Mayor Lawrence Deger ran Short and other gamblers out of town. Bat, Wyatt Earp and other gunfighters went to Short's aid. The two sides resolved their differences without a shot being fired, and Short was restored to his Long Branch Saloon.

In a picture, the gunfighters called themselves the "Dodge City Peace Commission." They disbanded on June 10.

From left to right, standing: William H. Harris, Luke Short, Bat Masterson, William F. Petillon; seated: Charlie Bassett, Wyatt Earp, Michael Francis "Frank" McLean and Cornelius "Neil" Brown.

George Hearst was the father of magnate publisher William Randolph Hearst and great-grandfather of Patty. In 1882 George and his partner friends visited mines in the Tombstone area, New Mexico, and Sonora, Mexico.

The local newspaper reported on January 3, 1882, that George was still a dweller in Tombstone and corrected a *San Francisco Exchange* report that George was in New York. On January 19, he left with J. H. Jackson and Geo. A. Berry for a new camp at Point of Mountains. George later came in from the Winchester District and was highly pleased with the outlook. George and Mr. Heyman Solomon purchased a group of five mines there, first discovered and located on the main ledge, and built comfortable quarters for their workmen. The mines showed rich chloride and horn silver ore.

In February, rumor had it that George and his party had been killed in Mexico. Fortunately, it was not true, and his party returned safe to Tombstone on Sunday, February 19. His party had visited Arizpe and spoke with the superintendents of the El Garchi and Carmen mines. They also went to Bacuachi before returning to Tombstone. George then went to the San Pedro Mine owned by John Sevenoaks, and this story included that George was the "most prominent democratic candidate for governor of California." On February 23, he left with J. H. Jackson and A. H. Stebbins to visit the mines of Victorio, New Mexico, and then to San Francisco.

16

The *Tombstone Epitaph* ran an article on March 7 that George "used to tell the following good story, which he said was good because there is so much human nature in it. Capt. Meacham, of Oregon, was one day traveling with a party of men when they were surprised and attacked by Indians. The captain was mounted on a rather docile, slow-going mule that did not at first rise equal to the emergency, and his comrades, who were better mounted, ran away from him. The captain shouted after them with all his might, 'Hold on there, hold on – we can lick hell out of 'em!' to which encouragement no attention was paid. Directly old muley caught a sniff and a sight of the Indians at the same time, when he started off at a furious pace that soon left the balance of the party far in the rear, when the captain looked back over his shoulder, shouting at the top of his voice, 'Come on, boys, come on – there's a t.h.o.u.s.a.n.d of 'em!'"

After San Francisco, George was back at Tombstone's Grand Hotel on April 4 in time to see General Sherman's arrival. A story exists that George wanted his picture taken at a saloon and hired it for an hour to get the picture done.

General William Tecumseh Sherman – General of all the American armies. Plans for his arrival to Tombstone started on April 4, 1882, by a committee composed of the mayor, council members, and local citizens. 100 local men were appointed to handle finances, reception, decoration, music, speakers, carriages, and hotel and hall reservations. Everyone in town was asked to decorate their houses and places of businesses. The mayor and others would meet the General at the Contention railroad station, and the fire department and various fraternal societies would meet him at the outskirts of the city to form a processional escort through the principal streets to the hotel. The line of march was up Allen to Third Street, then to Fremont to Sixth Street, then back to Allen Street and then to the hotel.

However, on April 7, a telegraph was received that General Sherman's party would arrive that night! His party consisted of Generals Willcox and Poe, Colonels Morrow and Perry, Captains Haskell and Smith, and Misses Sherman and Poe. Tombstone hurried to make everything ready. The party, in two six-mule ambulance conveyances, arrived to a cheering multitude, firing of salutes and music by the band. The mayor stepped out on the hotel balcony to introduce the General who made a short, impromptu speech. He said his throat was dry from the Arizona dust,

17

but he was happy to see so many fine looking, intelligent citizens … "above ground." The party then went to supper at the Maison Doree.

The grand reception was held the next day at 7:30 p.m. at Schieffelin Hall. A great many citizens gathered to shake hands with the "Hero of Atlanta," and he seemed glad to see everyone. His party left the next morning for Fort Huachuca.

John Ashworth Crabtree, Jr., was the brother of the famous singer and actress Charlotte Mignon "Lottie" Crabtree. In the June 1880 census, he was a 23-year-old miner in Saw Mill Flat, California. He met Annie Leopold's mother who became his housekeeper, and her family lived with him. Annie was 14 years old and got pregnant. John went to Tombstone in August 1880 as a mine prospector; Annie joined him later. She was introduced around town as his wife.

George Whitwell Parsons met John in August, but didn't like him much. In October John's mother bought the Kentucky mine and an interest in Ed Bullock's livery for him. The baby girl was born on March 19, 1881. John left Tombstone sometime after October 14, 1881. He had just returned from Sonora, Mexico, when he was summoned by his mother Mary to come back East and help Lottie as her stage agent. The baby was abandoned when Annie left Tombstone around March 26, 1882, and she was brought up by John's partner Ed Bullock and his family.

John was a worthless man who lived off Lottie for years and died in 1920 in North Carolina of liver disease. After Lottie died in 1924, her estate was valued at $4 million. Many "heirs" showed up in Boston including Annie's baby now married with the name Carlotta "Lottie" Cockburn. Even though Wyatt Earp and other Tombstone citizens claimed her right to be Lottie's heir, the court denied her.

LET'S HEAR IT FOR THE GIRLS

Women in business June 1880, published in September 2020

Just a year into the steady migration into Tombstone, the census population was at 3,000 and was predicted to reach 5,000. Miners came by droves. Businesses sprang up quickly in tents while waiting for buildings to be erected. Men were butchers, bankers, attorneys, doctors, grocers, and owners of saloons and hotels. Women, too, ran clothing and food stores, restaurants, and hotels. They were seamstresses and milliners. Some were teachers, and one was a doctor.

Here are the names of the businesswomen and comments from *The Weekly Nugget* newspaper of June 1880. (Pardon, but the list does not include the well-known "ladies of the night.")

Allie Earp, Virgil's wife, said she insisted on bringing her sewing machine to Tombstone in December 1879. On arriving, she saw the need for tents, and she and her sister-in-law Mattie, Wyatt's wife, began making them. They charged a penny a yard and made a great big tent out of canvas for a saloon. Both 22 years old, Allie was from Nebraska, and Mattie was from Wisconsin.

Mrs. Smith ran her restaurant near the Cosmopolitan Hotel. "A small house with a good run of transient customers and boarders."

Mrs. Mary Toomey ran the Bodie Restaurant on Allen Street. "A comfortable dining hall, and boarding house." She was 29 from Ireland.

Mrs. Lucy Young and Belle Sullivan owned the Star Restaurant. Lucy was 33, Belle was 36, and both were from Ireland. "They have fitted their

hall up in the neatest style for comfort and luxury, and have a splendid and expensive outfit of table wares and furniture."

Miss Nelly [sic] Cashman (see picture) was a "dealer in boots, shoes, hosiery and ladies wear … a specialty of gentlemen's furnishing goods. She has a neat store, well filled with a select assortment of goods…"

Mrs. A. L. Warren (Emma) on Allen Street was a "dealer in fruits, confections, farm products and choice family products … she will make a specialty of keeping full and constant supply of fresh butter, eggs, cheese, vegetables and California fruits." She was 27 from California.

Mrs. Leonie C. Holley ran the Rural House on Allen Street. Leonie was 32 from Pennsylvania and married to John. "This dining hall is one of the choice places, being suitably and pleasantly arraigned, and is kept as a first-class dining room."

Mrs. Ruth J. Brown and her daughter Lois on Fourth Street did "dressmaking in fashionable style, plain and fancy sewing, etc." Ruth was 44 from Kentucky, and Lois was 17 born in California.

Mrs. Peters also did dressmaking on Fourth Street and was the "agent for celluloid goods of all patterns, collars, cuffs, shirts, etc."

Two ladies Cosper & Tasker on Fremont Street built an adobe building for a store. A. A. Cosper was 38 from Pennsylvania, and Marigold Tasker was 52 from Vermont. They stocked it with "ladies furnishing goods and fancy wares ... every article in the line of bonnets, hats, feathers, trimmings, embroideries, laces, buttons, etc." They also did millinery, dressmaking, sewing and embroidering.

 Mrs. C. S. Fly (see picture) worked with her husband Camillus in his photography studio. "One feature that attracts the attention of all who visit his place is the display of colored photographs. These are the handiwork of Mrs. Fly, and cannot be excelled." Mary called "Mollie" was 32 from Illinois.

Mrs. S. E. Fallon came to Tombstone in early 1879 from San Jose, California. She was 22 and born in Canada. She erected the San Jose House which had twenty rooms comfortably furnished. It was being run by Miss Francis Jackson. Mrs. Fallon was currently the proprietress of the Ladies' Furnishing Emporium on Fremont Street. "All kinds of ladies', children's and gents' hats. Gents' large silk handkerchiefs. Ladies' corsets, all sizes, cheap. All kinds of millinery, plumes, feathers, etc., etc."

Mrs. Marion Webb, M.D., had her office at the corner of Sixth and Fremont streets.

Miss McFarland became the public-school teacher upon Miss Lucas' retirement in March. The newspaper reported that the unruly boys will toe the mark "particularly as we have noticed upon her desk a 'persuader' that never tires in the hands of a good strong person."

Other businesswomen were: Carrie Hanson, age 39 from Denmark, a hotelkeeper; Fannie Fulkerson, age 32 from Ireland, a hotelkeeper;

Catharine Kilillea, age 30 from Ireland, a dressmaker; and Johanna Leary, age 27 from Ireland, a confectionary maker.

A nice homage was paid to women in the marriage announcement of Catharine Ghilati and Charles Brown on March 25, 1880. "Everything looks brighter and better at the Mohave hotel already, as the touch of a bright, cheerful woman in apartments where batchelors wont to dwell, is like an oasis in the desert. Sunshine takes the place of clouds."

Kilkenny Cats, published November 2020

The fable of the Kilkenny cats is that two got into a ferocious fight, and at the end, only their tails were left. Absurd? Quite! But the metaphor continued for years denoting those who fought ferociously to their ruin – or as a symbol of tenacity and spirit.

During the Civil War, Ulysses S. Grant used the metaphor to say the North would win because it had the longest tail. This was depicted in *Harper's Weekly* on June 25, 1864. George Gordon Meade made the same remark in a letter to his wife.

Tombstone had its own version of the Kilkenny Cats in 1881. On the night of July 24, Mrs. Margaret Keegan, age 39, and Mrs. Ellen McKenna got into a fight. Mrs. McKenna owned the boarding house on Fourth Street (although the title was in dispute,) and she was evicting Mrs. Keegan for non-payment of rent.

Mrs. Keegan was absent from the house when Mrs. McKenna and three male friends went to the premises and proceeded to throw her furniture, trunks, bundles, and boxes out of the house. Mrs. Keegan returned, and the *Epitaph* wrote: "the row began, and Donnybrook fair wasn't a circumstance. In the melee Mrs. Keegan got her arm fastened in the door, and the screams were uttered which alarmed the town. Several hundred men were soon on the spot, along with the police, and all the belligerents were marched to the police station."

Mrs. McKenna was arrested for disturbing the peace. The *Epitaph wrote:* "Like an old veteran she plead guilty and was let off with a fine of $20 and costs amounting to $17.50, making $37.50." The *Daily Nugget* wrote that she paid her fine and "sailed out of court like a fifty-four-gun frigate going into action."

Mrs. Keegan was arrested by Marshal Earp for disturbing the peace. However, "on motion of the City Attorney, she was dismissed, as in his opinion she had been more sinned against than sinning."

The *Epitaph* continued: "during Mrs. Keegan's enforced absence at court yesterday, her landlady, the belligerent Madam McKenna, had some of her retainers go into the house in dispute and pitch the contents out into the back yard and lock the doors, thus obtaining a peaceable(?) eviction."

However, Mrs. Keegan's went back to the house, and the *Daily Nugget* wrote that "the crowd present were treated to an airing of dirty linen as only a couple of old and angry women, familiar with each other's family history, could give."

No more was written about the Kilkenny Cats. In the 1882 Tombstone census, they had moved away. Mrs. Keegan and her daughter Rosannah moved back to Florence, and Mrs. McKenna moved to nearby Contention.

Emma Parker – Soiled Dove, published in April 2022

Emma Parker was what Tombstone called a "soiled dove." She came to Tombstone in its early years and was listed in both the 1880 national census and the 1882 Tombstone census. She also was in the newspaper quite a lot having a rather fractious and fighting nature.

In the 1880 census, the soiled doves can be identified in that they lived alone or a few together, and they had the occupation of "Keeping House." Married women in town also had the occupation "Keeping House," but they were listed underneath their husband's name and before their children if they had any.

Why become a soiled dove in 1880 Tombstone? Perhaps, her parents were deceased, and she had no other family or skills to provide an income. Or perhaps, she was extremely unhappy at home, had no prospects for marriage, and decided to run away. A few were actually lured with false hopes of a job, only to find out, the job was prostitution.

Emma was born in 1852 in New Jersey. In 1880 Tombstone, she lived with Jennie Pomroy who was born in 1860 in California. They lived on Allen Street and were the 76th "dwelling house" to be surveyed. On one side was a Chinese couple who did washing, and on the other side was William Chamberlain, a carpenter, and Henry Fry, a miner. The population that year was 973.

Trouble seemed to come Emma's way often. When she purchased a house and lot on Allen Street, the March 5, 1881, *Tombstone Epitaph* wrote:

... [it] was and is occupied by Emma Burns, another soiled dove, as it were. Emma the first gave Emma the second notice to move out, but the latter had evidently resolved herself into a land league all by herself and didn't propose to be evicted. Yesterday, s. d. No. 1 went to the house and not only fired out through the front door all of s. d. No. 2's worldly goods, but did also bite the said Emma's left ear. Whereupon recourse was had to Justice Wallace for a warrant, and Emma Parker is now $32.50 worse off even than before, by reason of a fine imposed by his honor and paid by the finee."

Emma Burns was born in 1850 in Missouri. The land league referred to above is a take-off on the Irish Land League which was helping oppressed, poor farmers back in Ireland. Our Emma, s. d. No. 1, was also charged with assault with a deadly weapon, but the case was dismissed on May 26. More trouble came to Emma in the devastating June 22 fire. The fire destroyed several blocks and over 70 businesses, and Emma valued her loss at $3,000. The fire started in front of the bar of the Arcade saloon on Allen Street in a condemned barrel of liquor. Either a match was lit or one of the workers was smoking a cigar. When the barrel was opened to measure the volume, the escaping gases ignited causing an explosion of the liquor. Not three months later, more trouble came to Emma. Tombstone had passed laws in April which included License Tax No. 2. All kinds of businesses, including billiard tables for hire and nine or ten pin bowling alleys, paid $10 per quarter. Peddlers paid $10 per month; and dances, shows, and exhibitions paid $2.50 per night.

Emma's September 20, 1881, License for a House of Ill Fame still exists, and it was sold in 2016 for $9,500. Receipt #592 was for $4.30 for a term of thirteen days (monthly fee $10.) It was signed by Mayor John Clum on the front; however, it was canceled as she refused payment. The selling price at auction was so high because Virgil Earp signed the non-payment notice on the back.

On September 28, the *Tombstone Epitaph* wrote that Emma would be prosecuted in Wells Spicer's recorders court for keeping a house of ill repute. However, the trial was moved to Police Court before Justice Albert O. Wallace on October 1. The jury could not agree and was discharged. Once more trouble came to Emma on October 12, but this was her own fault. The *Tombstone Epitaph* wrote: ... she strayed into the Occidental Saloon at an early hour this morning, considerably under the influence of border benzine, and made such a nuisance of herself generally that the aid of a policeman was solicited by the proprietors of that symposium. On the appearance of the official, the gentle Emma gave vent to such ear-piercing vociferations as would have caused one of Tiffany's pets to turn green with envy. She now languishes in durance vile, and will be afforded an opportunity to explain her conduct before the proper authorities today." Again in front of Justice Wallace in Police Court, Emma pled guilty to the charge of drunk, disorderly, and resisting an officer. She was fined $20 and costs amounting to $7.50, all of which were promptly paid.

"Tiffany's pets" was a reference to Col. Joseph Capron Tiffany, and his "pets" were the Apaches on the San Carlos Reservation. Tiffany had succeeded John Clum as Indian Agent there. And John Clum, who now was editor of the *Tombstone Epitaph,* was exaggerating when he used the phrase "durance vile" – lengthy imprisonment.

The new year 1882 was just as hard on Emma. On March 6, 1882, she filed a lawsuit against Gus Williams to recover a watch and chain. This time she went before Justice Andrew J. Felter. The jury agreed with her and rendered a verdict for the plaintiff.

Then in April, Emma shelled out a lot of money to own three lots in Tombstone. She was caught up in the Edward Field's lawsuit against the Tombstone Townsite Company organized by James Clark and Michael Gray. Field's mine, the Gilded Age, was under part of the town of Tombstone, and he wanted everyone evicted or they should pay him for their lots. The Townsite Company had already said the lots were sold to those living on them. It looks like Emma decided to pay off everyone and get full title to the below lots on 6th Street and Allen Street on April 10, 1882:

Jas. S. Clark et al., to Emma Parker lot 8, block 6, $1

Jas S. Clark et al., to Emma Parker, lot 20, block 20, $600

Maggie Crumblish et al., to Emma Parker; lots 20 and 21, block 20, lot 8, block 6, $3000.

Edward Field et al., to Emma Parker, lot 20, block 20, lot 8, block 6, $1,000

Emma's lot 8, block 6, is now part of Tombstone's City Hall complex, and her lots 20 and 21 on block 20 across Allen Street are now the Tombstone Wine Works.

On September 2, 1882, Emma was out $300 for making a loan to Mrs. Inez McMartin who skipped town with her paramour, Joe Price. Mrs. McMartin actually mortgaged her effects twice, the other to J. S. McCoy for $200. On top of that, Mrs. McMartin then quietly sold the twice mortgaged effects. Several merchants were also left "holding the bag."

Emma filed one more lawsuit against Hugh Haggerty in November. Born in 1844 in Ohio, Hugh was a miner. However, the details and the outcome of that case are not known, but Hugh lived in Bisbee in 1884.

Emma must have moved to Benson because, on January 28, 1888, she was overdue for the $6.61 tax on Lot 27 block 20 and improvements for a total value of $200.

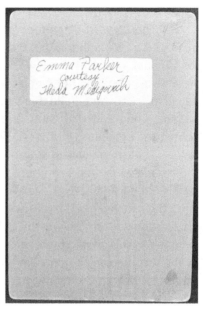

A picture of Emma sold for $45 on July 9, 2015. It was sold by J. Levine Auction & Appraisals which is now out of business. On the back of the picture is the name Theda Medigovich. She was born in 1910 and died in 1984. Together with her husband Samuel from Yugoslavia, they ran a plumbing business in Bisbee in 1940. They came to Tombstone in 1945 and ran the Wagon Wheel Restaurant for 12 years. She was a great collector of Tombstone memorabilia and opened the Silver Nugget Museum and Gift Shop. She was also president for a time of the Tombstone Restoration Commission. So, I think the above photograph of Emma is probably the real thing.

Nothing further was found about Emma Parker. Life had not been easy for her in Tombstone, but it seems she made quite a bit of money and was a property owner. She lived through the growth and decline of the silver mines, the many gunfights like the O.K. Corral, and more than likely, the scorn of the other women. Like it or not, the soiled doves served the needs of the miners and other men in the years when men greatly outnumbered the women in Tombstone.

The following women were performers in Tombstone.

Nellie Boyd, published in May 2020

The *Tombstone Epitaph* and *Nugget* newspapers didn't agree on much, but In December 1880, they both definitely agreed that the Nellie Boyd Troupe of entertainers was first-class. Nellie was known as "the versatile artiste," and her company was called "sterling." Although they played in Tombstone in Ritchie's Hall without much scenery and props, audiences flocked to see them and many performances were sold out. The troupe was excellent whether performing tragedy, comedy or farce.

The troupe was to stay for just one week that year, but because of packed houses every night, they stayed another week. The *Epitaph* wrote: "So worthy a company as this should be repaid for their trouble and expense in coming to this remote corner of the earth for the people's entertainment ..."

On November 29, their first performance was *Fanchon, the Cricket*. Local musician Mendel Meyer led the orchestra. *Fanchon* was repeated another night and was also performed as a Saturday matinee. In addition to the plays mentioned in the ad, others were: *The Rough Diamond, The Octoroon, Solon Shingle, Lady of Lyons* by Bulwer (a great dramatic play), *Bought or Lost and Won, Kathleen Mavourneen and Nan,* and *Good for Nothing. Two Orphans* was repeated because many could not get in to see the first performance. In *Ticket-of-Leave Man*, Nellie played a male character. This was known as a "pants role."

The troupe's last performance was a benefit for the Tombstone Hose Company No 1. It included the plays *Dora or the Farmer's Iron Will* and *The Fool of the Family* with locals performing the Highland Fling. The performance was mired by a few hoodlums acting up. Tombstone's benefit

> # THEATER!!
>
> ### RITCHIE'S HALL,
> ### For a Short Season Only.
>
> THE VERSATILE ARTISTE
>
> # NELLIE BOYD,
> #### Supported by the Superb
> ## DRAMATIC COMPANY,
> ##### COMMENCING
> # Thursday, Nov. 29.
>
> REPERTOIRE OF PLAYS:
>
> CASE FOR DIVORCE,   TWO ORPHANS,
> TICKET-OF-LEAVE MAN,
>   CELEBRATED CASE,
> FANCHON,   EAST LYNNE,
> . ROSE MICHEL, CAMILE,   CASTE,
>   AND MANY OTHERS.
>
> Admission,   -   -   -   - $1.00
> Reserved Seats.   -   -   -   - $1.50
>
> For Sale at Levi's Book Store, No. 432 Allen St.

for the troupe the next night included the play *The Hidden Hand* with music by locals Mendel Meyer on violin and Miles Kellogg on guitar. During the benefit for her, Nellie performed her favorite piece "The Lady of Lyons."

Nellie's repertoire included 21 pieces. Her emotional acting brought tears to the audience especially as Louise, the blind girl in *The Two Orphans.* The *Epitaph* wrote her acting was so "natural and true to bring tears to many of the fair as well as of the sterner sex." She was "thoroughly a mistress of every part she plays" and was known for doing "unrivaled impersonations."

During *Octoroon,* the *Nugget* noticed a sway in public opinion. Two scenes contained discourses on mob rule and lynching. The audience applauded the monologue against lynching and was silent during the one that promoted it. The *Nugget* wrote that this was significant to show the "disposition of our people for law and order." An octoroon is a person who is one-eighth black by descent. The play was a popular melodrama with the heroine committing suicide in the end.

The troupe stayed at the Cosmopolitan Hotel. Maggie Boyd is listed as part of the troupe, and Nellie did have a sister named Maggie who was eight years younger than her. Unfortunately, on December 12, actress Little Georgie was burned after coming into contact with a hot stove at the hotel. Events in Tombstone during their stay included a daring robbery of a man in a buckboard of $736, Marshall Ben Sippy offering a $10 reward for the return of his lost revolver, and the moving of Judge Reilly's house into the street by the "Clark-Gray gang" over a disagreement of land ownership. Interestingly, a mine south of Charleston was named "Nellie Boyd."

HOTEL ARRIVALS.

AT THE COSMOPOLITAN.

F. Roper, M. B Donahue, T. H. Bermar, G. Dupshur, W. Griffin, San Francisco; A. Walsh, Calistoga; A. B. Wood, Chicago; George Bridge, Mrs. Wiggins, J. Duncan, Wm. Herring, J. Dyer, Bisbee; E. Hogue, Empire City; A. Pritchet, Smartsville; Nellie Boyd Dramatic Company, consisting of Miss Nellie Boyd, Miss Maggie Boyd, Miss Florence Clifford, Miss Jennie Darrough, Little Georgie, Geo. Welty, O. L. Hart, S. Philleo, Harry Emery, and Warren Noble.

The troupe returned in February and in December 1881 for an engagement at the recently built Schieffelin Hall. Now, they had the scenery, props, costumes, and stage to perform the plays correctly. They did *The Banker's Daughter* which had run for 200 nights in New York City, *Forget Me Not, Celebrated Case, Hazel Kirke* which had already achieved the mark of 1,000 consecutive performances, *A Case for Divorce, M'liss, Kathleen Mavourneen* as a benefit for Tombstone's Irish Land League, *East Lynne,* and *The New Magdalen.* They held a small concert on Allen and Fifth Street their second day to advertise their plays.

The *Nugget* wrote "... the Nellie Boyd Company has won the esteem of all of our citizens, not only by their professional merits but also by their gentlemanly and ladylike deportment…" The troupe arrived just five weeks after the O.K. Corral shooting. During their stay, the "Cow-Boy Scourge" was the topic of the day with Governor John J. Gosper and Galeyville residents writing their complaints to the U.S. State Department. Cow-boy Curly Bill and three of his gang were in Charleston that week "making it lively," and five cow-boys were hung in nearby Shakespeare.

Nellie Boyd

Nellie was born Ellen/Helen Birney in Pennsylvania around 1848 and moved with her family to Chicago ten years later. Nellie said she first took to the stage at age 16. In the 1870 Chicago census, she was listed as 22 years old and an actress. She made her New York City debut in 1876 as Ned Compo (a "pants role") in the Booth's Theater production of the *Flying Scud*. In the spring of that year, she performed in the Lyceum Theatre. During the next three years, she performed in Baltimore, Chicago, Cincinnati, Pittsburgh, St. Louis, and many towns in Kansas. Plays' names were: *Off the Stage, Round the Clock, Lemons or Wedlock for 7, Blue Glass, Big Bonanza, The Mulligan Guard Ball, My Son,* and *Comedy of Errors*. She worked primarily in Augustin Daly's company.

Nellie Boyd.

Nellie organized her own traveling troupe in 1877-78. The troupe toured in Kansas, Montana, Nevada, Utah, and California before coming to Arizona in November 1880. In Arizona, the troupe performed in Tucson, Tombstone, Phoenix, and Prescott.

A professor visiting the Bird Cage Theatre a few years ago saw a poster and wrote: "… a yellowing sepia poster of a very proper-looking lady in a bustled gown staring unashamedly at me. The print was labeled 'Nellie Boyd Company.' She was holding a parasol in her small leather-gloved hands and her dark bangs curled out from under a bonnet. Her dress seemed to be of an expensive satin and a fashionable design."

In Prescott on Christmas Eve 1880, some young men disturbed the theatre during acts, and she was also robbed of $1,000. Afterward, the troupe went to New Mexico. Nellie had two managers during these early years. John W. Toohey left the troupe in January 1880 and was replaced by George Welty.

In the spring of 1881, the troupe performed in many New Mexico, Nevada, and Arizona towns. They returned to Arizona again in December 1881 and in August 1883. In 1884 in Seattle, Washington, Nellie's program for *Claire and the Forge Master* was a real keepsake. It was printed on satin with a fringe border, tied with a double bow knot, and scented on a cabinet card.

The following years, the troupe played in Kansas, Montana, Alabama, and New Orleans. Nellie decided to retire in 1887. She moved to Fresno, California, with her aged mother. Nellie bought a 40-acre vineyard and became active in many women's clubs and organizations. She helped collect raisins for the World's Fair in 1900 Chicago and also donated pomegranate fruit from her orchard. She was named to the State Educational Commission in 1900. She helped with the local high school's performances and graduations, and at times, would leave Fresno and perform professionally. In 1888 she played in *Passions Slave* and *His Natural Life* in Sacramento. One of her last performances was in the musical comedy *The Burgomaster* in New York City. She played Mannie Fair. It ran from December 31, 1900, to January 26, 1901.

In the summer of 1900, Nellie's sister Mrs. Martha Edger Berry had surgery in San Francisco. A few months later, Martha came from Chicago to visit Nellie in Fresno. Sadly, Martha died of pneumonia at their mother Margaret Birney's house on August 21.

Nellie died unexpectedly of a heart attack at her home on Elm Avenue on November 6, 1909. Her funeral was done under the auspices of the Christian Science Church. In 1893 Nellie had signed a deed that when she died, all her property would go to her mother. However, before the deed was delivered to her mother, she died twelve days after Nellie at the age of 88. Nellie's other sister Mrs. Margaret Northcraft and husband James owned a 240-acre ranch in nearby Riverdale. Margaret was the administratrix of Nellie's estate and inherited her cash and property. Nellie's brother John, born around 1853, was a farmer in Fresno. Nellie was predeceased by her father John, born around 1821, and brothers Hugh born in 1852 and Henry born in 1858.

A manager and friend of Nellie's wrote a long article about Nellie in the Fresno paper. Thomas R. Harrold told of her goodness and love for people.

Miss Nellie Boyd.

Once while traveling during her last season of 1886-1887, they came on school children trapped in their schoolhouse during a blizzard. Nellie sent the stagecoach on to Boise City, Idaho, for food and supplies. The troupe took their robes to the children, and then razed a nearby barn and burned the wood to warm the children. They then entertained the children singing songs and telling stories until the supplies returned at 9 p.m. The troupe spent the night with the children.

Thomas closed his article with this: "She seemed to live for and took the greatest pleasure in giving pleasure and comfort to others. It came so naturally to her to spread the sunshine and gladness. That is why Nellie Boyd was so well beloved by the people."

Peake Sisters, published in June 2020

The Peak Sisters.

The entertainment to be given next Friday evening at the Schieffelin Hall by "The Peak Sisters" will be of rare amusement to our people. Ten Spinsters whose opportunities for enjoyment in life have been very much suppressed, start out upon an exhibition tour under the guidance and direction of the eldest sister whose quaint efforts to show off the accomplishments of her sisters from the playing of a Jews' harp to singing operatic airs, furnish the drollest and funniest situations imaginable. The sisters are accompanied by their own orchestra, and the instrumentation shows what wonderful effects can be produced by a tin trumpet and a penny whistle in artistic hands, or rather, we should say, artistic mouths. Those who wish to secure a comfortable seat should early procure tickets, which are to be had at Pata's Drug store, Sol. Israel's and Brown's Book store. Tickets 50 cents.

The October 29, 1880, *Tombstone Epitaph* newspaper announced the coming of the Peake Sisters to the monthly concert and social at the Presbyterian Church: "You will never forgive yourself if you fail to attend ... Betsey Bobbett and her poetry; Swanee River with the combicon accompaniment, and a dozen other things (including the sisters) all 'too good for anything.'" Combicon? What's that? Tombstone's other paper, *The Daily Nugget*, reported that no men were in the troupe – and "an indignation meeting is in order." The Peake Sisters returned to Tombstone in April 1887 and played at Schieffelin's Hall.

A pamphlet detailing the performance was arranged by Mary B. Horne in 1887. The ten sisters/spinsters were described as wearing black dresses with white cuffs and white aprons. Their large white handkerchief had the letter P in one corner, and their white cone hats were two feet high with black bows on the top. They all held fans and band boxes of proportional sizes to their height. Every movement was done precisely and in unison, especially when standing up to take a bow. They would stand, turn around, place the band boxes on their seats, turn to face the audience, and bow until their caps touched the floor. They would then turn again, take up their boxes, and sit.

The eldest and tallest sister Keziah was the narrator who introduced the other sisters. Dorothy had vocal lessons at a preservatory (i.e., a cool place to store food.) Bethia, a cultured Boston girl, wore blue glasses. Maria lived on a farm in the western part of the state and was very practical. Betsy, who once spoke to a man, was deaf and dumb, yet performed her part perfectly and lipped the songs. Sophia was the smallest who was adopted during the group's travels. She was hired when the group heard her high soprano voice calling her folks to dinner. She was the imp of the group who was the only one allowed to smile and speak out.

Their favorite musical instruments were big black combs covered with tissue paper -- the combicons! They also played the Jew's harp, tin trumpets and penny whistles. They toured from the Rocky Mountains to China – Pek-in (get it?) The family was reared in the "peaks of Alaska," and when the U.S. purchased Alaska, their mother decided to take her daughters on tour for entertainment. Their mother had since returned to Alaska.

In the program, Sophia refused to sing the "Old Maids' Song" with the others. She then sang a song about her honey who will buy her everything: a nice piano, a thousand-dollar watch and chain, a diamond ring, and a nice new dwelling upon the avenue. Maria recited a poem "A Rhyme of the Time" to poke fun at Bethia from Boston. In the poem, Miss Pallas Eudora Von Blurky was highly educated, spoke many languages, knew why Shakespeare was wrong in his grammar, but Miss Blurky "didn't know chicken from turkey."

Keziah closed with "If you wish to raise money again to paint the church, or to carpet the vestry, or to pay the minister, just send for us. Still there are times when we think of mother in the land of the Peaks, and almost wish that the United States had never purchased Alaska. We led a free and easy life there – no cares and no culture." To the tune of "Old Folks At Home," they all sang:

> Way down upon the Alaska River, far, far away
> There's where our hearts are turning ever, there's where the
>   Peaks all stay.

There they ride on reindeer sledges, wearing hats like these;
And there they coast along the edges, and do just what they please.
Miles on miles from that far river, wanderers lone are we.
O mother, how our hearts turn ever, back to the Peak's land
    and thee.

Even their ads announcing their arrivals were funny. Performances were to start "precisely at eight o'clock and fifteen minutes." They had just performed for the "crowned heads of Europe, Asia and Africa," and their "costly instruments were of rare construction." One newspaper reported that one sister would be able to perform since her broken heart was patched up by Professor Roentgen's Z rays. Another newspaper reported that they were still in town "not having enough money to pay their tavern bill and other damages … and they would soon leave on a tour of Patagonia and the Fiji Islands."

Other Towns and Local Actors

Newspapers as early as 1874 carried notices of the Peake Sisters performances. They played in Chicago, Illinois, and in Omaha, Nebraska. Their performances were well-received and then copied by local troupes to raise money for churches and civic organizations.

In April 1879, a local troupe of "Old Maids" was in Carson City, Nevada. They returned in September and played at Moore's Theatre. This troupe consisted of: Minnie Blackburn, Annie Martin, Emma Smart, Fannie Parkinson, Mrs. Howe, Flora Schneider, and Mollie Ackley. Their songs included "Alasky State Forever" and the staple "Muffin Man."

In September 1879, the Oakland newspaper called them an "amusing burlesque." On their return four months later, the newspaper labeled the entertainment as "rich, rare and racy." Mrs. L. S. Clark was in charge, and the troupe was called the Peake Sisters of Alaska. In San Francisco that month, they wore the traditional costumes of black dresses, white kerchiefs, white cuffs, and peaked hats. The newspaper said they were "most novel and unique … held the audience in the most [unreadable] and genuine laughter and enthusiastic delight. Each number was a new surprise." In December 1881, the program's title was "The Peake Sisters from Alaska Town or After a Mate."

Local performances continued into the 1890s and beyond. This picture is of a local group in 1895 in North Turner, Maine, courtesy of the Turner Museum and Historical Society.

In 1902 Vancouver, the performance was labeled a "musical mélange and olio of oddities." Local troupes performed as late as 1922 in Hydro, Oklahoma. Revival shows, based on Mary Horne's pamphlet, were done in Vevay, Indiana, in April 2016.

Nellie Hyslop

Nellie Hyslop was one of the "sisters." In 1895 she performed in Waukau, Wisconsin, on the same night the depot almost burned down. They were at Pomeroy's Hall situated over Weyman's blacksmith shop when their program was interrupted until all the bucket brigadiers returned. Nellie gave the newspaper an interview for Waukau's 1946 centennial celebration.

She said her costume was a black dress with pointed white cuffs, a pointed white apron, and a 12-inch high pointed white hat. The "sisters" came out with extravagant introductions, did a march which incorporated peaking around each other to carry out the implications of their name. Part of one of the speeches was "A little nonsense now and then is relished by the wisest men." The sisters played "Yankee Doodle" and "Home Sweet Home" on combs covered with tissue paper. A couple of sisters whistled a duet.

Nellie was born in Wisconsin in 1864, lived in Waukau in her later years, and died there in 1957. Her parents were from Scotland. She had an eighth grade education as did most children during that time. In 1916 at age 52, she married James Hyslop, a butter maker in a creamery, but she was divorced by age 64. In 1930 she was working as a nurse for a private family.

Early Beginnings

A connection seems to exist between the Peake Sisters and the Peak Family. The latter began touring the east coast as Swiss Bell Ringers in 1848.

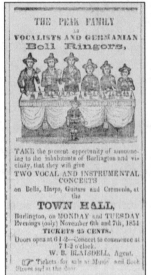

Sometimes, the name was spelled Peak, sometimes Peake. The family consisted of music professor William Henry and his wife Mehitable, 16-year old daughter Julia, 7-year-old daughter Fannie, and 17-year-old son William, Jr. Their shows were warmly received and provided not only music but fun.

Father William reportedly saw a Swiss bell ringer group in Eastport, Maine, at a P. T. Barnum show. The group was returning to Europe, so William bought their bells and self-taught himself. In 1850 Pittston, Pennsylvania, Fannie was described as having a "fairy like appearance." Her brother sang tenor, and her father sang bass.

It is possible that the daughters exaggerated the costumes when they began touring as the "Peake Sisters." The cremonia in the ad was probably a small violin named after Cremona, Italy, where violins were first made by Andrea Amati in 1542 and 1546. W. B. Blaisdell, the agent named, was married to Julia Peak.

Admission was always very reasonable, and one time, the performance was free. The group played in New Orleans in 1869. Father Moynihan of St. John's Baptist Church and school brought 700 children to the performance thinking it was free. The group's agent agreed to charge $70. But Mr. Peak told him not to charge at all. Father Moynihan was building a church, and if he paid the $70, he would, in turn, ask for a $100 donation for the church. The agent agreed!

By 1879 this ad from Somerset, Ohio, shows the combination of the Peak Family of Bell Ringers with the Nine Old Maids from Alaska. It was advertised as "astonishing exhibitions – musical and unmusical – wise and otherwise..." A few times when the Peake Sisters performed later on, the act included some bell ringers, too.

The children were all born in Medford, Massachusetts, and their parents were born in Charlestown. Three other children were Edward A. born 1847, Charles born 1849, and sister Lizzetti born 1852. Edward died at age 5 months, and Lizzetti died young, too, in Cleveland. Another son named Eddie S. performed with the family in 1873 and died in Nevada at age 20.

Father William trained many new bell ringers who then organized their own troupes. His Peak Family troupe made thousands, but he spent most on touring, donations to charity, and gifts for his children. He also lost money in gold speculation and investing in a theatre in the early days of Pike's Peak.

By 1885, William was 76, destitute, and living with his wife in a poor house in Homer, Pennsylvania.

In 1867, the Peak Family troupe split with Julia and brother William Jr. touring west of Ohio, and the rest of the family touring in the eastern and southern states. Julia, her husband William Blaisdell, and their son Willie were in the troupe that performed in the Atchison, Kansas, show of 1872. In 1885, Julia and her family lived in California. Sister Fannie had married a wealthy Southerner John Fitch who lost his property after the Civil War. He died shortly thereafter. In 1885, Fannie lived in Jamestown, Dakota, with her son and daughter. She had interests in the lumber and hardware business.

The Peake Sisters and the Peak Family performed hundreds of times across the nation. Their arrivals were always highly anticipated, and their performances never disappointed. They provided wholesome, fun enter-tainment and were always invited to return. Others learned to perform like them enabling this amusing entertainment to reach even more audiences.

Star Novelty Troupe – Patti Rosa, published in August 2020

In early May 1880, Tombstone hosted hilarious and "clean" performances by the Star Novelty Troupe. The troupe held eight evening performances and a matinee performance on Saturday May 8. Thoughtfully, the troupe held the matinee for miners who worked the night shift and for children. A benefit was given for the troupe on May 13 at Eaton & Rice's. Locals Gus Lee, a 29-year-old bartender from Illinois, played his banjo, and Andrew Robertson, a 38-year-old saloonkeeper from Scotland, performed his great Highland Fling in complete dress.

Coy and flirtatious, Patti Rosa was the "Star" of the troupe. Known as "the beloved soubrette" and as "the talented little soubrette," she was

heralded as being the next Lotta Crabtree. Like Lotta, Patti was piquant and pretty and had a bright smile. She sang, danced, played the hornpipes and banjo, and was a "champion Lancashire clog dancer." Her dancing included kicks and "peculiarly knowing winks." Patti was hired by San Francisco's Bella Union in early 1880 to tour California and the Southwest. She later toured the southern states and the east coast in many musical comedies.

The first one called "Chance" was performed in Lincoln and Omaha, Nebraska. The *Omaha Daily Bee* on November 19 reported she was an impish mischief-maker on stage, and her voice was a sweet mezzo-soprano. Another comedy called "Mizpah" was performed in Philadelphia in 1884, and she performed in "Bob" in London, England, in 1889. Returning to Arizona, she starred in "Imp" in 1891 in Tucson and Phoenix, and "Dolly Varden" in 1892 Tucson. Patti was born in England, and her mother was the famous Madame Cerito known for her "transformation dance." Patti died in 1894 after an appendix operation. She was just in her early 30's and was looking forward to an upcoming engagement in Boston.

Frank Roraback led the company of "Stars." His rich tenor voice made him popular on the Pacific coast. In November 1879, he was part of Pauline Markham's English Opera Company that performed the "H.M.S. Pinafore" in Tucson. He played Rackstraw, and the newspaper called him a "graceful and careful actor" who "throws himself into his part with warmth and fidelity." After touring with the Star Novelty Troupe, he went back to the Bella Union in December 1880.

Other "Stars" in the troupe were: Robert Scott, Dave Boothby, and Fred F. Brooks. Robert was Patti's husband, and he performed eccentric songs and funny sayings with Negro/Ethiopian being his specialty. Dave Boothby performed as a German character "Fritz Von Hozensloger" and also did Irish burlesque. The Tombstone newspaper called him another Gus Williams, a local Tombstone man who was a judge at the horse races on November 26. Fred Brooks was known for his great Shakespearian and tragedian skill. His recitation was called "Jim Bloodsoe/Bludsoe."

Professor Paul Louis Boulon was the leader of the troupe's orchestra. He was known as the greatest violinist on the Pacific coast who also did imitations of birds and bagpipes. In Prescott that July, he played "The Sleigh-Bell Polka." In April 1876, he and his musical family left Walla

Walla for Boise and California. His wife Noonie played violin, piano and brass instruments; his sister Emily was a cornetist and alto player; and his father Louis Leander played violin and cornet. Paul was born in France in 1847 and died in California in 1907.

Besides Tombstone, the Star Novelty Troupe played in Tucson that April and again in mid-May. Songs performed in Tucson were "Darling, I am Growing Old" and "We are 62 Tonight." Other stops in Arizona were at Charleston, Harshaw, Phoenix, and Prescott.

All the newspapers were very complimentary after the troupe's performances. Everyone seemed to especially love Patti Rosa. After Patti's performance in Tombstone, J. H. De Wees and E. Dickerson located a mine in the Tombstone District and called it the "Great Patti Rosa and Liberty." There is even a Patti Rosa mine in the Cripple Creek District of Teller County, Colorado.

TOMBSTONE CITY BAND

TOMBSTONE CITY CORNET BAND

"TOMBSTONE MUSICIANS"

Tombstone Musicians in the Early Years,
published January through April 2020

A honky-tonkin' piano player is a staple in all western movies. What would a saloon be without one? In the early 1880s, Tombstone had its piano players, too, but it also had a medley of other musicians who played at parties, dances, socials, festivals, holidays, funerals, and church services. Professional, traveling musicians came to Tombstone and performed at Ritchie's Hall, Schieffelin Hall, and the Bird Cage Theatre.

The most notorious musicians in Tombstone were the "accordion fiend" and the "trombone fiend." The *Tombstone Epitaph* reported on August 4, 1881: "The accordion fiend and the careless discharger of firearms have been consigned to the deepest dungeon." The other newspaper *The Nugget* reported: "Accordeon [sic] to a statement in our contemporary, the fiend who plays the sleep-destroying and murder-provoking instrument in this neighborhood, will be cremated promptly at 6 p.m. to-day, and his infernal machine turned over to the Chinese band." The next day, a published letter from Horatio Collins to Mr. Cook disagreed that the accordion music at 2nd and Toughnut "come o'er my ear like the sweet south wind breathing upon a bed of violets." A week later, the *Nugget* reported that the fiend still lived, but "the vengeance of an outraged and long suffering community awaits him." The accordeon fiend was finally sentenced one October day. However, the trombone fiend was still at-large and "opened fire on the *Epitaph* office last night. It is to be hoped he will take warning by the fate of the accordeon fiend whose doom was sealed yesterday in Police Court. If he does not, he will be consigned to Hades without recommendation to mercy."

Besides those "fiends," Tombstone had many good musicians. Noteworthy piano players during the early years were: John Charles Willoughby, Emil Rehbein, Charles Nathaniel Pring, Mrs. Alson Emery (Kate) Ingersoll, Mrs. Brown, and Mrs. E. S. Irwin.

John Charles Willoughby, who was 25 years old, played piano at the Oriental Saloon. The Oriental was infamous for its gambling and for the killing of Charlie Storms by Luke Short in February 1881 and the killing of Billy Claiborne by "Buckskin Frank" Leslie outside it in November 1882. Charles resigned as pianist in December 1880 as he was "seized with prospecting fever."

39

Emil Rehbein ran a private music school in Tombstone. Both he and Mr. Willoughby played at the benefit for Budd Philpot's widow and children. Budd was a stagecoach driver who was killed during a robbery attempt on March 15, 1881. The benefit collected over $700.

Charles Pring was a 28-year-old miner from England whose wife Gertrude died in Tombstone in September 1881. Both Charles and his wife were associated with several productions of the "H.M.S. Pinafore" in Tucson and at Tombstone's Schieffelin Hall. At Tombstone's Fourth of July program in 1882, Charles played the organ. He was also the organist at the Episcopal Church, and he repaired and tuned both pianos and organs.

From Pennsylvania, Mrs. Ingersoll, age 28, was married to a 33-year-old dentist from Illinois. They had moved from Montana where their two children were born; Elenore was now 6 years old, and Thomas D. was 4. Mrs. Ingersoll was the pianist for the "Grand Floral Concert and Mythological Exhibition" at Schieffelin Hall on May 5 and 6, 1882. A benefit for the Presbyterian Church, this musical was about the coronation of the Arcadian queen and included songs by milkmaids, farmers, gypsies, and nymphs. In "Part Third," Mrs. Ingersoll played a waltz by Frederick Chopin.

Mrs. Brown and Mrs. Irwin both played in the program presented by the ladies of the Methodist Church on October 18, 1881.

Mendel Meyer

One of the most well-known musicians and entertainers was Mendel Meyer from Prussia. Mendel was just 5' 3.5" tall but was full of energy and fun. He was 42 with black eyes and hair, had an oval face with a dark complexion, and had a scar on the center of his forehead. He came to America around 1859 with his brother Samuel. Naturalized in Los Angeles in 1871, Mendel was a clerk and dry goods merchant there and was well-known for giving social parties and annual balls. On July 16, 1880, he held his first ball in Tombstone at Danner and Owens' hall. An expert violinist, he included a piano in his orchestra that night. The *Epitaph* newspaper reporter composed a 14-stanza poem after the occasion including the lines:

> *"... the strains of the Blue Danube echo through the crowded hall.*
> *Jove! The music is delicious, is the verdict of them all.*
> *Waltz and quadrille, polka, schottische, followed in an endless rune,*

*And the women looked so charming; blonde and demi-blonde,
and brune ..."*

The last line read: "All voted it a grand success, a first-class, bang-up ball." Note: A quadrille is a square dance, and a schottische is a slow polka.

On July 27, Mendel played at Captain Henry Malcolm's party in nearby Watervale, and on August 6, Mendel gave a ball in Tombstone with two violins, a cornet, and a piano playing "all the latest fashionable music." Mendel went to Los Angeles for several months but returned in November 1881. He played nightly "musicales" at Benjamin Wehrfritz's Eagle Brewery and also played at the Manhattan Club's socials for the season.

Mendel's next ball was given on December 23 at the Turn-Verein Hall with Miles Kellogg's band furnishing the music. Three days later, Mendel's band performed at the Grand Holiday Ball at The Meyers House in nearby New Contention.

Mendel and the Italian string band played at the 5th anniversary party for Mr. and Mrs. Julius A. Kelly on February 15, 1882. The *Epitaph* reported that the music included "the entrancing harmonies of harp, violin and flute mingling sweetly with the rhythmic movements of the dancers and the subdued murmur of the happy voices."

Grand Holiday Ball !

—AT—

THE MEYERS HOUSE,

New Contention,

Monday Evening, Dec. 20.

THIS WILL BE THE FIRST BALL GIVEN by the proprietors at the new hotel, and no pains will be spared to make it a most enjoyable affair. A cordial invitation is extended to all.

Music by Mendel Meyer's Band of Tombstone.

Parties who may come by private conveyance are assured that their teams will be carefully attended to.

TICKETS (Admitting Gentleman and Ladies, including Supper).............$4 00

The Italian string band played at the Head Center Mine party on March 17, 1882. It was a send-off for Messrs. C. S. Batterman and M. A. Elliott who were leaving for San Francisco. The newspaper wrote: "A space in the hoisting works between the engine and the main shaft had been cleared and tastefully decorated with flags and bunting. The floor was smoothed and well waxed, and a raised platform erected for the musicians..."

The Italian musicians at the time were: Frank Lobracco, age 22, his brother Rocco, 26, and Joe Califero, 24. Rocco worked at Pasqual Nigro's Comet Saloon, and Frank later was the proprietor of the O.K. Corral and livery in 1883. On February 15, 1882, Frank was one of the musicians at the Knights of Pythias' Ball. He had just returned with George Hearst from a mining expedition to Basochuca, Arizpe, Sonora, Mexico. Frank, Rocco, Joe along with Pasqual Nigro, Antonio Dufemio and D. B. Jones owned a copper mine there.

Mendel dabbled in mining, too. He went to relocate his mine in the Dragoons on January 1, 1883. That night while camped, he and another man heard their horses run off, presumably by Indians. Mendel said that he walked the four hours back to Tombstone and met some desperate-looking Sonorians on the way. Although he had $300 on him, he told them he was broke and hungry, and they gave him a tortilla to eat. However, since he was a known entertainer, not everyone believed his story.

Miles Erastus Kellogg

Like Mendel Meyer, another expert violinist and party-giver was Miles Erastus Kellogg. A 44-year-old from Ohio, he ran The Diana dance hall, saloon, and lodgings in Tombstone at 316 Allen Street. His quartet of "skilled musicians" was available to play at balls and social parties.

> **THE DIANA**
> **Lodging House and Saloon.**
> Next Door to Gray & McLan's Corral.
> M. E. KELOGG, : PROPRIETOR.
> Best Brands of Liquors & Cigars.
> **SINGLE BEDS, FIFTY CENTS.**
> Rooms to Let.

As early as 1860, Miles had listed himself as a musician in the federal census of Omaha, Nebraska. Gold was discovered in 1868 in Elko, Nevada, and the next year, the newspaper reported that Elko had 100 saloons, 16 gambling houses, and two hurdy-gurdy houses. Miles lived in Elko then with Conrad and Margaret Repp who ran a local hurdy-gurdy. Conrad was a 26-year-old saloonkeeper from Germany. Lizzie Foy, a 20-year-old hurdy-gurdy girl from England, lived with them. Other hurdy-gurdy girls in Elko were all from Germany: A. Weaber, age 16, C. Hillibrant, 30, and S. Krone, 18.

Hurdy-gurdies were a well-known staple in western mining camps. Typically, a married couple hired four girls, traveled to a new mining camp, and opened up a dance hall. The miners would pay to dance with the girls to the music of a small band which usually included a piano and a violin. The girls were strictly chaperoned during the evenings of dancing. This picture is a typical hurdy-gurdy from the website petticoatsandpistols.com.

Miles was part of the Elko Glee Club which played at the benefit for Miss Frances Honeywell in February 1870 at the courthouse. The other club members were Mssrs. Vincent, Brown, Gonne, Steinberger from Germany, and a 30-year-old from Illinois, J. W. Hess. An Italian boat song began the concert. These songs, also called barcarolles, were very popular then – something a gondolier would sing in Italy. The group also performed a song called "Fairy Doll." Later, they played at the first weekly lecture series of the Elko Debating Club and at the Fourth of July program, too.

UNION BAND.

THE UNION BAND IS NOW ORGAN-
ized and prepared to furnish brass and
string music for all occasions. Apply at Dan.
Morgan's saloon.   M. E. KELLOGG,
d6   Business Manager.

In December 1874, Miles had moved to Eureka, Nevada, and was the business manager for the Union Band. He was active in politics and was Eureka's representative to the Republican convention in October 1876.

By July 1879, Miles had moved to Prescott, Arizona, and his Quadrille Band included guitarist Olliver Trevillion, George Vogt, a 23-year-old from New York on double bass, and banjoist Walter Beam. While in Prescott, a painting was done of Miles and another singer, a Mr. Davenport.

PRESCOTT QUADRILLE BAND

Is now organized and will furnish Music for

**City and Country Dances, Pic-
nics, Serenades, Etc-**

The Band consists of the following pieces.

M. E. KELLOGG   Violinist,
O. TREVILLION   Guitarist
GEO. VOGT   Double Bass,
WALTER BEAM   Banjoist.

Leave all orders at GEO. YACKLE's, Montezuma street
Prescott, A. T.   Jy13tm

Silver was discovered in Tombstone, and in late June 1880, Miles and his partners located a mining claim called the Panama in the Lee District. His partners were both 21 years old: L. S. Karns and F. H. Buckles who was a cook from Illinois. On March 20, 1881, Kellogg, Morris, and Bishop McDaniels bonded the Parnell mine for $40,000.

Miles lived on Allen Street in Tombstone and opened The Diana dance hall, saloon, and lodgings. The newspaper reported that on July 4th, "flags and streamers were displayed from nearly every building," and Miles' decorations along with other saloons and hotels were noted as being "profuse in ornamentation." The newspaper reported that The Diana held a "good dance in good company," and everyone could have "the best music and a delightful time every night." The Diana held a social party with Kellogg's full string band.

The Diana or "Kellogg's Hall" hosted many private events, too. On September 6, Mrs. Josie Harcourt gave a ball there attended by merchants, doctors, lawyers, miners, and mine experts. On October 23, another ball/social hop was held at Kellogg's. A grand ball was held at The Diana located "next to the Dexter Stables" the next August. It was originally

43

scheduled for Zumer's Hall but had to be moved. In March 1882, a fancy dress or masquerade ball was held at The Diana.

Kellogg's was mentioned in the trial of the October 26, 1881 shooting at the O.K. Corral. Cow-boys Billy Clanton, Frank and Tom McLaury were killed in the gun battle. Virgil and Morgan Earp were wounded. Billy's brother Ike Clanton was unarmed and ran from the fight. He went through the O.K. Corral, across Allen Street, into Kellogg's saloon, and then to Toughnut Street. Their fellow Cow-boy Billy Claiborne, who also ran from the fight, said he had left his gun at Kellogg's the day before.

Miles and his bands were very popular and in demand. His string band serenaded the *Epitaph* newspaper staff on the evening of September 3, 1880, and the quartet was thanked in the newspaper the next day. On September 29, the Tombstone Social Club gave its first social at Ritchie's Hall with Kellogg's band playing the music. The *Epitaph* reported that the club was made up of "the most prominent in social and business circles," and the entertainment would be "in every particular recherche." (Recherche means exquisite or rare.)

On October 28th, Kellogg's "unexceptional" (meaning no equal) band played at another Tombstone Social Club party at Gird's Hall attended by 25 couples, and the band played for the Club's Thanksgiving party at the Grand Hotel on November 25.

When Myron H. Kimball was leaving for Los Angeles in December, Kellogg's cotillion band serenaded him at his office. Myron was a 54-year-old mining operator from New York. Members of the band that day were: Mendel Meyer, Doc-Robb March Thompson, a 52-year-old harness maker from New Jersey, and Harry L. Bailey, a 40-year-old carriage painter from Belgium. The *Epitaph* reported: "The serenaders were invited in and treated in right royal style." Probably, a few drinks were served all around.

On March 25, 1881, a benefit was held for the widow and children of the murdered stagecoach driver Budd Philpot. Miles played his guitar in a duet with his friend Gus Lee on banjo. The benefit, which collected over $700, included many singers, dancers, instrumental music, and a skit.

Gus Lee was a 29-year-old bartender from Illinois. The previous December, he lost his silver-mounted banjo between Pick-Em Up and the slaughter house. The *Nugget* reported: "The finder will be liberally rewarded by leaving the same at the Diana saloon. It is the property of Gus Lee, and he is lonely without it." Gus was an early arrival to Tombstone, and he played with the Star Novelty Troupe in May 1880 at Eaton and Rice's. Gus ran the Criterion Saloon and Restaurant with Arthur Britton, a 27-year-old from Ohio. Arthur skipped out with all the assets leaving Gus to "face the music" on July 30. Gus' quadrille band played on August 10 at a private party at the Cosmopolitan Hotel dining rooms. The *Epitaph* reported "… until the wee sma' hours the devotees of Strauss, led by Lee's quadrille band, drove care to the winds." In 1883 Gus was the barkeeper at Hafford's saloon.

Just like Gus, not all was fun and gaiety for Miles either. In November 1880, probably needing money, Miles sold a bathtub and water tank, capacity 160 gallons, for a "low price." The next July, The Diana establishment was assessed at $200, and on October 16, Miles was found guilty of keeping a disorderly house. This meant he did not keep the yard clean around The Diana. He and the townspeople pled for mercy, but he was ultimately fined $77.50. Finally, due to whiskey and bad management, all Miles' bar and lodging fixtures were auctioned off in March 1882.

On Sunday, June 4, 1882, Miles and his partner Bob/Joe Young provided the music at the Fireman's Picnic at Kendall's Grove and the Grand Ball at the Meyer's Hotel in Contention. Their five-piece band at the picnic included two violins, a clarionet, a guitar, and a bass viol. The picnic included foot races, dancing contests, and a baseball game. The *Epitaph* reported that the musicians were excellent. They played at the grand ball until early the next morning. The newspaper reported that on Wednesday Miles drank too much and felt weak on Thursday. At 4 p.m. he "passed to the unknown shores of eternity."

Miles, a bachelor, was buried in Boothill. At his funeral, a parting dirge was played by his musician friends: leader Edward Wittig, tenors John and Emil Schmidt, James T. Duffy on tuba, Harry L. Bailey on B coronet, and Charles Edwards on bass drum.

Edward Wittig was 41 from Germany. He served in the Missouri 5th Cavalry from September 1861 to September 1862. In Tombstone he was a teacher of both vocal and instrumental music. John H. Schmidt was 58 from Germany and was naturalized in September 1858 in St. Louis. His son Emil was 16 from Missouri. (When John died on May 1, 1884, grocer Joseph Hoefler became Emil's guardian. At Emil's marriage that year, Miles' old Prescott friends Olliver and Mrs. A. Trevillian were witnesses.) James T. Duffy was 34 from New York, and Charles Edwards was a 37-year-old engineer from England. Later that year in August, James Duffy was the leader of the band at the Bird Cage Theatre. A fire broke out on Fremont west of First Street, and James was able to save most of his property. A spark or lighted cigar stump was thrown carelessly away at Mrs. Mooney causing $2500 in damages. Fellow musicians Edward Wittig and John Schmidt lived nearby.

Miles' estate consisted of 50% ownership of lot 5, block 3, known as 316 Allen Street, and an old dilapidated frame building currently rented out as a saloon. It adjoined Dunbar's livery stable on the east. His possessions valued at $111 were: four bedsteads and straw mattresses, three tables, a parlor and bar room stove, a bar room counter, a small desk, a watch and chain, a ring, and a tool chest. No heirs were listed.

Other Bands

On July 1, 1881, the *Nugget* reported that the new Tombstone Brass Band was out last night at the Bonanza Saloon. The band was also called the Vincent Band for its leader Thomas Vincent. They serenaded the public at times and played at the Ice Cream Festival for the benefit of the Baptist Church Sunday School on July 22. On July 28, the *Nugget* reported favorably on the "proficiency achieved by our local band." The band had just paid $60 for a new bass drum from New York.

All band members were from England. Thomas Vincent on 1st coronet was 29 years old, Frank Garland on 2d coronet was 27 and a miner, George Eddy on 3rd coronet was 31, and H. Trevina was on 4th coronet. Charles Winslow was on 1st alto, and 26-year-old miner Richard Goldsworthy was on 2nd alto. Richard Fuzina was 1st tenor, John Pidwell was 2nd tenor and 27 years old, and Mr. Young was on 1st trombone. Frank Bread was on 1st baritone, Mr. Butler was on 1st E flat baritone, and William H. Vincent was on 2nd E flat baritone. William was 36 and proprietor of the Music Hall Saloon at 529 Allen Street in 1883. Samuel/Sampson Simmons, a 23-year-old miner, played bass drum. No one yet played the tenor drum. Other members at times were: Harry L. Bailey, Leslie F. Blackburn, age 39 from New York, Edward R. Peacock, a 42-year-old painter from Kentucky, and Julius A. Kelly, a 29-year-old saloonkeeper from Los Angeles. Edward and Frank R. Randall, age 30 from Ohio, had the Council's contract to do the street lettering and house numbering in November 1880. House owners paid 50 cents per number.

October was a very busy month for the band. They played at the reopening of the Oriental Saloon, performed a "literary and musical programme" for the Methodist Church ladies, serenaded a rich miner George Warren Atkins who then bought them all a new hat from Glover's store, and led the funeral procession for those killed at the O.K. Corral.

The new year 1882 started off with a grand parade on January 2. The Tombstone Brass Band led the parade from the firehouse on Toughnut Street. Engine Co. 1 came next with its decorated engine and its mascots "mose" and "lize" who were played by 12-year-old Miss Lottie Moses and Master Norman Woods. The Rescue Hose & Ladder Company came next. Its truck was "tastefully adorned and carrying the Goddess of Liberty" played by Miss Nellie Rafferty. (Note: The Statue of Liberty was currently under construction in New York City.) The overhead canopy was ornamented with stars and stripes. Edward Peacock had just repainted the engine after losing a bet on the recent election of the new fire chief. At the end of the parade, the firemen visited each other's firehouses.

The Tombstone City Band (see page 38) gave a social party on February 4 at the Turn-Verein Hall. Councilman J. M. Nash presented leader Thomas Vincent with a gold medal. The next day, William Vincent, leader of the brass band, was also given a gold medal made by the local jeweler, Herman Schmieding.

Over the next few months, the band played often at Schieffelin Hall. Vincent's string band played at the Knights of Pythias ball on February 15. The room was decorated with "different emblems of the order, over the stage was woven in evergreens the word 'Welcome,' while at the entrance was suspended an elegant silk flag of the Union Rank of the order. Some twenty canaries were placed in different parts of the hall whose sweet and merry voices added to the music and the pleasure of the evening." At 9:30 p.m., the Grand March was held followed by the first quadrille dance of the evening.

On February 22, the band played at the grand ball of the Solomon Lodge of the F. and A. M. Masons. "The floor was well waxed and was all that could be desired by those who delight in tripping the 'light fantastic.'" The supper was provided by the famous restaurant, the Maison Doree. On March 17, Vincent's string band played at the St. Patrick Day grand ball given by the Sons of Erin. Two beautiful flags, one Irish, one American, made by the Sisters of St. Joseph of St. Louis were presented to the Redpath Branch of the Irish Land League in support of the cause of freedom for Ireland. On May 12, Vincent's band played at the Grand Social Necktie party given by the ladies of the Catholic Church.

The band played at other noteworthy events that year, too. On April 7, they played for General William T. Sherman's arrival. He came with General Orlando B. Willcox, General Orlando M. Poe, Colonels Henry A. Morrow and Perry, Captain Haskell, Miss Sherman, and Miss Poe. A Grand reception was held at Schieffelin Hall the next night. This picture is from the *Sacramento Daily Record-Union* of 12/16/1882.

MEN OF THE HOUR.

GENERAL WILLIAM T. SHERMAN.

A few weeks later, some Apaches had left the San Carlos Reservation and were raiding and killing settlers. A call went out for volunteers to meet at the Grand Hotel on May 1. Vincent's brass band played at the gathering of Tombstone citizens. Those who had a horse or mule were asked to volunteer for a 60-day campaign against the Indians. Captain Mike Gray was to be in charge.

As always, July 4 was a day full of activities, and the festivities included music by the Cornish Brass Band/Tombstone Band and Charley Pring on the organ.

The next year, on August 11, 1882, the Tombstone City Band played as the new courthouse cornerstone was laid. The cornerstone was hastily put into position as it was pouring rain. Inside the cornerstone are the names of the Tombstone City Band along with coins, business and legal documents, ore specimens, a bulletin of post office regulations, poems, essays, and a cigar.

Another band active in 1881 and 1882 was the Tombstone City Cornet Band. (See picture on page 38.) On August 4, 1881, George Frederick Spangenberg, the famous gunsmith, reported preparations for the Turn-Verein ball were going well, and the string band of the City Cornet Band would play. He said the floor may be canvassed which would "prove an attraction to many devotees of Terpsichore." On December 22, the newspaper announced that the Tombstone Cornet Band was to play the next week for Madame Du Pree's six-day pedestrian contest. She was an athletic walker who challenged all comers to this contest. At the end, she had walked 454 miles with locals Joe German walking 146 miles, Phillip Hope 157 miles, Sam Barron 90 miles, and G. V. Spann 48 miles. Madame won the contest by walking 13 miles more than all the others put together.

On January 4, 1882, the Tombstone Cornet Band led a midnight victory procession. The band went to the homes of Mayor-elect John Carr; councilmen Charles N. Thomas, E. H. Dean, Thomas A. Atchison, and J. M. Nash; chief of police David Neagle; treasurer Heyman Solomon; and recorder A. O. Wallace. Each was woken from sleep and led to Hafford's corner to celebrate with a drink. Next, they went to the Delmonico House, and with the tune "St. Patrick's Day in the Morning" playing, out came Nellie Cashman. Then they all went inside to tables full of food and drink.

Another band in Tombstone in March 1881 was called the Silver Independent Cornet Band. It was

Silver Cornet Band.

The Cornish miners, who have so often delighted our citizens with their vocal music have organized a band to be known as the Tombstone Independent Silver Cornet Band, under the leadership of Prof. Rosewarne, late of Sonora, Tuolumne County, Cal. The following is the membership: Prof. Rosewarne, 1st Eb cornet; Frank Garland, 1st Bb cornet; Henry Trevena, 2d Bb cornet; Richard Goldsmith, 1st Eb alto; Richard J. Trezona, 2d Eb alto; J. H. Gregory, 1st Bb tenor; G. Eddy, 2d Bb tenor; Frank Brand, Bb baritone; John Martin, Bb bass; J. E. Butler, Eb bass; Sampson Simmons, bass drum and cymbals; Richard Trezona, Secretary

48

composed of Cornishmen as was the Silver Cornet Band. The newspaper wrote that this latter band, organized on April 23, 1881, was composed of the Cornish miners "who have so often delighted our citizens with their vocal music..."

Led by Prof. John Rosewarne on 1st Eb cornet, age 47 from Sonora, California, the members were: Frank Garland, 1d Bb cornet and a 28-year-old miner; Henry Trevena, 2d Bb cornet; Richard Goldsmith, 1st Eb alto; Richard John Trezona, 2d Eb alto and a 24-year-old blacksmith; J. H. Gregory, 1st Bb tenor; George Eddy, 2d Bb tenor; Frank Brand, Bb baritone; John Martin, Bb bass; J. E. Butler, Eb bass; and Sampson Simmons, bass drum and cymbols. Messrs. Garland, Trevena, Eddy, and Simmons had also been in the Thomas Vincent band.

The Mexican brass band from Sonora, Mexico, played in Upper Tombstone on July 20, 1880. The band had been retained by Pasqual Nigro to play in his dance house. On November 13, he ran an ad for Pasqual & Bro musicians who were available to play at balls and private entertainment. Two years later on October 3, Pasqual was playing billiards with some others in his Comet Saloon when Maria Contreras ran screaming by and holding a towel to her neck. She had been stabbed by her ex-lover Jack Sanford who then turned the razor on himself. Both lovers died and are buried in Boothill.

A call went out in December 1880 for all musicians wanting to form a new band to meet at Kelly's Wine Rooms. Tombstone's Brass Band was formed at Kelly's on December 13: N. L. Bailey was the leader, Leslie F. Blackburn was the treasurer, and Edward Peacock was the secretary. Eight musicians were present, and Julius Kelly offered to contribute $50 for the purchase of instruments. Julius Kelly was a distinguished violinist. His saloon was mentioned in the trial of the O.K. gunfight. Ike Clanton was drinking at Kelly's that morning with Joseph Stumpf, a 34-year-old baker and miner from Germany. Julius fell ill in the fall of 1882 and went to the Huachuca Mountains for his health. The newspaper wrote that this "pioneer violinist has agreed to give one last performance at Schieffelin Hall on October 14."

Dances were held often in Tombstone, and on July 30, 1880, the Tombstone Quadrille Band played at a social dance, and in August, a Select Ball was held at Ritchie's Hall with music by Kirby & Co.'s Quadrille Band.

Various Tombstone bands led funeral processions to Boothill. Rancher James McMartin died 9/4/1881 of consumption. James Tulley died 10/5/1881 in a mine accident, and miner Frances Southy died 11/1/1881. The three Cow-boys shot at the O.K. Corral - Billy Clanton, Frank and Thomas McLaury - died 10/26/1881. Fireman John Ahearn died 12/27/1881, and Anton Weiner died 1/22/1882, both from natural causes. The Mill Restaurant proprietor Rufus Cowing died 2/2/1882, and store clerk William C. Bennett died 3/24/1882, both from heart disease.

Other musicians

The Pesquez Brothers arrived in Tombstone from San Francisco in October 1880. The *Epitaph* reported that they joined the Alhambra Saloon orchestra. The Alhambra was run by Thomas Corrigan at 433 Allen Street. Thomas, age 25 and from Ireland, had sold his mine for $40,000 and opened the saloon with the money.

O. W. Bauer and Daniel O'Connor were cigar and tobacco dealers on Allen Street. O. W. played the zither, and Daniel O'Connor played the guitar. On March 25, 1881, they played at Budd Philpot's benefit with Messrs.

Rehbein, Willoughby, Kellogg and Lee. On October 18, they played in a program put on by ladies of the Methodist Church. They were so good, they received an encore. At Mrs. Carrie Gregory's benefit on March 7, 1882, they played instrumental duets with Mr. Koch. The Zither Club performed the instrumental music at the Knights of Pythias' program at its lodge rooms on April 24.

On January 2, 1882, Tombstone witnessed "its most novel serenading party... paying homage to the fair ladies of Tombstone." The unnamed musicians were all on a large wagon and included three violins, two guitars, two cornets, an alto horn, and an organ.

Tombstone was one of the many mining camps throughout the West after the historic Gold Rush of '49. Miners worked long and hard, and they looked to the camps and towns for entertainment. Tombstone's musicians answered the call to entertain at saloons, dances, private music halls, and churches.

And as one newspaper earlier suggested: They did a bang-up job. Excuse the pun, Mssrs. Earp!

ALL THAT GLITTERS IS NOT GOLD – SOMETIMES, IT'S SILVER

Silver Mines, Murders and Monikers, published September 2021

In the early 1880s, Tombstone had its really big silver-producing mines like the Contention, Grand Central, Head Center, Vizina, and the Tombstone Mill & Mining Company which owned 200 acres of mining claims. Other notable mines were the Dean Richmond, Flora Morrison, Good Enough, Lucky Cuss, Mountain Maid owned by the Earps, Total Wreck, and Toughnut.

In the January 1, 1882, the *Tombstone Daily Epitaph* ran an article on the biggest mines. They posted over a $3 million profit since their inception in June 1879. Big dollars for the time as most employed miners earned $4 per day, sheriffs earned $40 per month, and a horse cost $50.

RECAPITULATION.	
Tombstone M. & M. Co	$2,704,936 33
Western (Contention)	2,708,144 39
Grand Central	1,050,875 30
Vizina	526,710 98
Head Center	191,520 52
Boston Mill	112,724 29
Corbin Mill	40,000 00
Ingersoll	15,000 00
Sunset	15,000 00
Total	$7,359,017 81
DIVIDENDS.	
Tombstone M. & M. Co	$1,100,000 00
Western (Contention)	1,375,000 00
Grand Central—Repayment	300,000 00
Grand Central—Dividends	300,000 00
Vizina	60,000 00
Total	$3,135,000 00

However, the mines also caused problems when Tombstone began to build its town. The Gilded Age was owned by Edward Field, nicknamed "The Duke." Around this time, Mark Twain's book *Huckleberry Finn* was published and included a "Duke" – a fraudulent character who preyed on the gullible and naïve. Such was Tombstone's "Duke." His mine ran under a part of Tombstone, and he took issue with Michael Gray and the Townsite Company selling lots above ground. Michael's Way Up mine was parallel to the Gilded Age and was forced to shut down. The issue didn't get solved until mining was basically over in Tombstone. Around 1884, many mines flooded, and then the Grand Central hoist and pumping plant was destroyed by fire in 1886.

And then there were the murders associated with mining. Colonel John Van Houten was killed on November 9, 1879, at the infamous Brunckow Mine. Martin R. Peel was an engineer for the Tombstone Mill & Mining Company and was shot by either Zwing Hunt or Billy Grounds during a bungled holdup of its office on March 25, 1882. Earnest Brodines and Jacob Endlich worked at the Mamie R mine until Jacob presumably shot Earnest with both buckshot and a .45 calibre bullet in June 1882.

Accidents at the mines were numerous, and a few were fatal. James Tulley died on October 5, 1881, after he fell 125 feet from a cart which was hoisted too high and tipped over at the Grand Central Mine. Also killed there was John Plate who missed getting into the cage and fell 200' to his death on May 17, 1882. Matthew Harris died on July 22, 1883, after accidentally falling 24' off the gallows frame at the Flora Morrison Hoist works. William Brokaw died on November 17, 1883, after falling 30 feet from a ladder in the pump shaft at the Contention Mine. Michael Hoarty was injured when the Head Center mine cage stopped short of the level. He put his foot out on a bar, and when the cage rose, he was trapped between the cage and the timbers. He died four days later on March 15, 1883, of peritonitis.

A Mine must be named

All those who flocked to Tombstone ached for finding silver and wealth. Some hoped including Silver in the name would somehow help. For example, mine names included: Silver Belt, Silver Bill, Silvercable, Silver Flake, Silver Locket, Silver Plume, Silverthorn, and Silver Wedge.

Looking over about 500 names in the Tombstone district, a few stand out. Surprisingly, some of the miners were very literate. They knew European and Biblical history. For example, mines were named:

Afghanistan, Belfast, Blarneystone, Cleopatra, Huguenot, Prince of Wales, Trojan, Troy, and Zerubabel. (Yes, Zerubabel was a real person!) They also knew their Greek and Roman mythologies: Apollo, Aurora, Diana, Hercules, Hesperia, Jupiter, Sirius, and Vulcan.

American cities were popular from east coast to west coast: Baltimore, Brooklyn, Chicago, Cincinnati, Cleveland, Omaha, Phoenix, Sacramento, and San Diego. And so were the states: Alaska, California, Colorado, Delaware, Kentucky, Maryland, Nebraska, Nevada, New York (or the Empire State) and Texas.

People were popular, too. Beside men's names, there were the brothers: Bro Johnson, Two Brothers, Three Brothers, and Jolly Brothers. The girls weren't forgotten either: Aunt Sally, Dolly, Fannie A., Jennie Belle, Laura Louise, the Mexican maid Chiquita, and Vixen. Hattie seemed to be a popular name during this time: (just plain) Hattie, Hattie Dillard, Hattie L. Wheeler, and Hattie May. Surprisingly, some miners named their digs for Indians: Apache Maid, Cocopah, Mingo Chief, Pocohantas, Red Cloud, Red Indian, and Washo Chief.

Miners liked American icon names, such as: Buffalo Bill, Bunker Hill, Dixie, Mayflower, Plymouth Rock, Sultana, and Uncle Sam. Holidays were remembered, too: New Years Gift, Valentine, Fourth of July, Christmas, and Santa Claus.

Animals, Birds, and Insects were duly represented with: Ground Hog, Octopus, Old Mule, Poodle Dog, Rattlesnake, Tiger, Wolverine, Wood Rat – Eagle, Nightingale – and Grasshopper.

When miners opened a second mine and couldn't think of another name, they named the second one #2 and/or chose to do opposites: Alpha and Omega, Big and Little Pedro, East and West Side, or the combination of Sunrise, Sunset and Sunset #2.

My favorites mine names are: Black Diamond, Dew Drop, Gold Buckle … and all the Stars: Morning, Evening, North, American, and Star of Venus.

And lastly, under the category of "What were they thinking?" – mines were named: Milquatay (a valley north of Campo, California,) Nabocklish (a real word!), Sams Trunk, and X.X.X. (not to be confused with today's movie ratings!)

Prospector's Lament, October 14, 1881
originally published in *The Tombstone Epitaph*
Republished June 2021

Tune – "Hat My Father Wore."

Composed and Sung by George Atwood.

Oft o'er the lofty mountains, I've packed a stubborn mule,
Well loaded with provisions and a well-known mining tool;
Down in some lonesome canyon my pan of dirt to try,
The result of which would make the stoutest heart to cry.

I wish these paper fellows that write about the gold,
Were in a place the Bible says is never very cold;
For they write about the lumps of gold, so very rich and big,
But they never write a gol-darn word, how hard it is to dig.

Once I owned a bronco, and I bought him for a song,
He wasn't very handsome, but he carried me along;
But now I punch my burro all up and down the hill,
For my bronco's gone to San Simon, to carry Curly Bill.

There's Supervisor[Joyce], and Sheriff [Behan], we know;
Joe Dyer, Chairman of the Board, and Tasker in the row;
Poor Tasker, he's the target, and when he votes one yes,
Why, Joyce and Dyer squat on him, and win the point, I guess.

There is a local doctor, of municipal fame,
His bills are something elegant, Cochise allows the claim;
But where he gets his items, himself can only tell;
The county is young, so let him go, his fate we can foretell.

The clerk of the Board – a friend of mine – we often have a talk,
On mathematics he's the boss, you all can take a walk;
How it was done, we all do know – "just multiply by seven –"
For he shoved Lib Hasting's bill clean through – 100 for 11.

We've just held an election, for a Chief Engineer,
The goings-on would make you laugh, they were so very queer;

Bill Ives, he lost through traitor's vote; now, foremost in the van
Steps out the boy we now endorse, his name is Danny McCann.

Now, Ed Schieffelin and George Atkins, too, two well-known mining men,
With hearts as big as buffalo's, no small potatoes, them;
They'd as soon give up one hundred, for any worthy say,
So may their riches never fail, and both live many a day.

The Indians gave us quite a scare, they came from very far,
The troops went gallantry to fight, but never won a scar;
Our Mayor organized a band of fighters true and grand
And drove the red skin sons-of-guns into another land.

Here is a little background on the people mentioned in the poem.

George Atwood, a merchant, was born in 1845 Maine. When he left Tombstone, he was given a large benefit send-off on October 12. That's probably why the poem was published two days later.

Curly Bill Brocius was an outlaw who was noted for his antics as well as his outlawry. His home base was in Galeyville.

In the original printing of the poem, the names Behan and Joyce were reversed in error. Milt Joyce, born in 1847, was owner of the Oriental Saloon. John Behan, born in 1845 Missouri, was the county sheriff who was involved in O.K. Corral shootout. Joe Dyer, born in 1856 Maine, was a miner. Joe Tasker, born in 1834 New Hampshire, was a general merchandise dealer and also a Supervisor of the Board.

On October 4, Dr. George Goodfellow presented a claim to the Board for $1092.50 and $1064.90 was allowed. He became quite famous for his knowledge of operating on gunshot victims.

Clerk of the Court – Robert J. Campbell, born in 1853 Ireland, was owner of the New Orleans restaurant. Edgar "Lib" Hasting, born in 1847 Massachusetts, was a shoemaker.

Bill Ives, born in 1845 Virginia, was a store clerk as was Danny McCann, born in 1856. They both ran for Fire Chief, and the one hose company all voted for Bill; the other for Danny. Danny won 105 to 93.

Ed Schieffelin, born in 1847 Pennsylvania, was the original founder of the silver mines in Tombstone. George Atkins, born in 1846, became very rich with his mines the Belle Isle, Copper King and a Bisbee mine near the Copper Queen. He gave $100 to the bank for townspeople to properly drape their houses when President James Garfield died.

LOST AND FOUND

Tombstone's Lost, Found, Strayed, and Stolen, published August 2021

During its early years, quite a few items were lost and found in Tombstone. Some ranchers worded their ads as "lost" or "strayed" knowing their horse or cattle stock were actually stolen, but no one wanted to stir up any more trouble than there already was. And those who found stock labeled their ads as "Strayed" indicating they weren't rustlers.

A found jackass and a lost bulldog. The jackass' saddle, bridle and blankets were found on Fourth Street. Could have been a disgruntled miner who gave up digging, or the owner could have been in a drunken stupor, was in jail, or lost them in a card game. Another Tombstoner lost his "thorough-bred English bulldog, white, low set, cropped ears, dirty buckskin face, well scarred (for he was a fighter,) narrow strap on neck." Poor dog.

Guns were typically left somewhere, and the owners couldn't remember where. City Marshal Ben Sippy lost his gun and offered a $10 reward for it in December 1880. Ben's time as marshal was short as by June 1881, a $3,000 error was discovered in his records and angry creditors came forward. He was on a two-week absence at the time, and yup, you guessed it, was never heard from again. In September 1881, a Colt forty-one calibre pistol was lost, and "the thumb-catcher was filed off." If found, return to the Sheriff's office. This was probably a cowboy's pistol, and not surprisingly, it was to be returned to their buddy Sheriff Johnny Behan.

Roads were a little rough back then especially the road between Tombstone and Pick em Up on the way to Charleston. A black handbag containing loaded shotgun shells was lost between Tombstone and the Pick em Up Saloon located about 1 ¼ miles from Tombstone. Can't go far in those days without a drink. A silver-mounted banjo was lost between Pick em Up and the slaughter house. The *Nugget* newspaper wrote: "It is the property of Gus Lee, and he is lonely without it." Between Tombstone and Charleston, "a Red Leather valise, containing a silk dress and ladies' underwear was lost." TMI (too much information)? We think so!

After the fire in late May 1882, quite a few Lost ads cropped up for: a fire insurance policy – yeah, you need that! – a barber's stool, a music box, a box of pictures, a turning lathe and two boxes of gunsmith's tools, a Masonic emblem to be attached to a watch chain, and a blackingbox with brushes, blacking and a wisp broom. Couldn't get a decent shoe shine and a shoulder brushing at the Oriental Saloon's tonsorial parlor without those last items!

Back then, it was acceptable for men to carry <u>pocket-books</u>. The *Nugget* remarked though that "Some of the best-dressed men carry the shabbiest-dressed pocket-books." John Pedrazzini lost a pocket-book between Tombstone and Benson. It contained private correspondence in Italian and a certificate for 70 shares of the Eureka Tunnel and Mine Company. He asked that if found, please send to A. Guindani, an Italian merchant in Contention City. It's possible that a Found ad ran the same time by John Roman of Tucson, but he described the pocket-book as a Russian leather satchel. An autograph album and letters bearing the superscription L. E. Aubury was found. Lewis was a 17-year-old miner who later became a mining engineer in California. He died in 1933.

<u>Money and other negotiables</u>. A wallet containing money was found at the O. K. Corral in December 1880. Three months later, they ran an ad that two horses were either "strayed or stolen" from the corral. Speaking of the O. K. Corral and the famous shooting on October 26, 1881, a lady who was "in the post office at the time, in her fright dropped a pocketbook containing one hundred dollars in currency." She went to her home at the Boston Mill. Bank checks were often lost and even stock certificates. In December 1881, one ad read 1250 shares to the Solomon Mine were "LOST or STOLEN."

<u>And those slippery pieces of gold jewelry</u>! I. M. Chenowith lost a gold locket with his initials on it. On one side was a dog's head with small diamonds in the collar, and on the other side, a ruby in the eye. Fan-n-n-cy!! A small American gold watch in a buckskin case was described in detail: "lost between Calisher's and the City Lodging House on the north side of the street between 8 and 9 o'clock." Miss Sue Santee, an elementary school teacher, lost her gold watch that had two photographs on the dial. Sounds pretty! John P. Clum, editor of the *Tombstone Epitaph* and postmaster, lost his gold match-box with pink gold quartz in corner, and monogram "J.P.C." on the side. . . "The box being a gift is specially valued." It was probably a gift from his late wife who passed away in December 1880. A rough quartz scarfpin was lost between Allen Street and the Schieffelin Theatre. Found

jewelry included: a gold hunting case watch found by Dr. A. E. Ingersoll, and a lady's gold earring found on Allen Street. The latter could be claimed at the Mint Saloon. Or if she was shy, send a guy!

A rather "tongue in cheek" ad entitled "Lost Strayed or Stolen" reported: "From Benson on the night of the 30th of December, 1881, a partner in the blacksmith and wagon-making business. When last heard from, he was visiting a beautiful young lady residing at San Pedro bridge. It is feared that, suffering from temporary aberration of the mind (caused by too much bliss) when he left the house, he has missed his way, walked into the river and been drowned. Any information tending to the discovery of Mr. W-d-l will be gratefully received by his sorrowing and grief-stricken partner and a host of anxious friends." This was probably Alexander Kent Waddell, age 42 from Nova Scotia, a carriagemaker. His first wife died in 1878 in Massachusetts. In 1886 he married Helen, and he died in Bisbee in 1910.

Lastly, body parts Body parts? Yup! An upper set of teeth was found and left at the *Epitaph* office on March 5, 1881. Then 17 days later, a human arm was found in the street and reported to the newspaper. Let's hope its owner was okay, and that the arm was quietly buried in Boothill. So, if you ever see a ghost on one of those Bird Cage Theater Ghost Tours, and he only has one arm and lower teeth, you'll know why!

Lot Jumping, published October 2020

In 1880 Mike Gray and The Tombstone Townsite Company laid claim to all the above ground property, a 320-acre plot, which encompassed pre-existing homes and businesses. Tombstone's first settlers felt they owned their lots and houses because they had already paid mineral-claim holders and other parties. The settlers did not want to pay twice, so a legal dispute started that lasted for several years.

On Sunday, February 29, 1880, it was rumored that the Tombstone Land Office would stop selling town lots. E. J. Smith reported to the newspaper that all the vacant lots on Allen and Fremont Street were jumped that evening – even the "sacred precincts of the graveyard were encroached upon." This graveyard was an early one that was located on the city block that now houses the Circle K. It is bounded by Safford, Bruce, Sumner and First streets.

59

The Townsite Company was given its patent in November 1880, but concurrently, the mining law gave exclusive control of surface land to a locator before a patent was issued. Edward Field, nicknamed "The Duke," owned the Gilded Age mine claim and thus the ground property above it. Evictions were published, lawsuits were filed against the so-called "squatters," and as soon as one lost his property, he would pick up and move on another lot. Also, because not everyone built on their lots, others would come in, claim the lot, and start building on it -- usually during the night.

Besides the jumping in the graveyard, two other stories of disputed property claims were: the house that moved, and to coin Lincoln's phrase, "a house divided against itself cannot stand."

The house that moved

December 4 was a very windy night. Earlier that day, (James S.) Clark & (Michael) Gray had their men pull down Judge James Reilly's fence and move his house part way into the street. Marshal Ben Sippy stopped them, and some men pushed it partially back. Lowery, the only occupant of the house, called George Whitwell Parsons, who lived across the street, to stay with him. It was all legalized, George was given a police whistle and laid down on a broken-down sofa. Wesley Fuller, a gambler and friend of the Clantons, volunteered to stay, too. The night passed comfortably enough. George wrote: "A couple of drunks during the night were fooling around, trying to find their way home probably, as one said something about the house being in the way." The next morning, a crowd was raised and "we all made a rush and in a very few minutes had the house back where it belonged. There was much enthusiasm." George was nicknamed "Trojan" for his part.

George himself jumped lots on January 17, 1881. He with engineer H. B. Howe and D. G. Heylmun took six lots, two each, just beyond the school house on the opposite side. George got the choice ones on the corner facing the Dragoons running back 120 feet. As the law required, George dug post holes and built his house in a few days.

The house divided

John Plesant Gray was Mike Gray's son. He said "Our home place was partly on Gilded Age surface. The line of the mining location just cut off one room, but the hallway leading to this room was outside the Gilded Age lines. So one day when I was alone at home, my folks being away on a trip to the country, there appeared at the front door the county sheriff and a deputy to serve a court order to give the sheriff possession as a receiver to our one room claimed by Duke Field! It was rather an odd situation. My father had anticipated this trouble and told me not to allow the sheriff any possession rights, so I told the officer I would resist any attempt to take possession and that he must stay out. I guess it was lucky for me that the sheriff seemed a little doubtful about his authority when I convinced him that the door of the room was not on the mining claim and his only entrance would be through the window. He retreated, and in a few days the court ruled against the Duke's surface rights to any land except the same piece necessary for working his mine. And so the Duke had made his last stand, and he disappeared for the last time from the Tombstone scene."

By the time everything was sorted out and legally decided, Tombstone was actually on the decline. Many moved away when the mines flooded. But for a while, property ownership kept the courts busy and was quite the "talk of the day."

Nugget ad   Epitaph ad

EVERYBODY LOVES A CIRCUS

Ryland Circus, published in July 2020

George Whitwell Parsons noted in his diary on September 22, 1880: "Circus in town. First one – Rylands I think. Civilization advances."

Famous on the west coast, the Ryland Circus played in many Arizona towns in 1880. George Ryland owned the circus, and his wife Madame Elena was the star of the show. She performed on the slack wire (or slack rope), did bareback horse riding, and performed with her seven trained dogs. She could ride the Globe while tossing balls and knives and twirling plates upon the ends of wands, and she could ride four horses at one time.

Other acts included Messrs. Emerson and Morino as bronco and horse riders, Master George as a clown and jester, "German Sampson's" great feats of strength, H. Carl juggler, Carl Duprez contortionist, Nodesto Gutierez acrobat juggler, Carmen Perez on the flying trapeze, and Victor Perez and Brothers from Paris and London. The animals included camels named Romeo and Juliet with baby Nellie, Jaco the monkey, and Captain the mule.

The circus held a parade through Tombstone the night before. A benefit performance for the public school netted $57.50 on Saturday, September 25. Oddly, the two newspapers in Tombstone ran different ads for the circus.

The Ryland Circus first played Arizona cities and towns in 1878. They returned each year through 1882. Major towns visited were Phoenix, Prescott, Yuma, and Tucson, and they also played in neighboring towns like Tempe, Florence, Fort McDowell, and Globe City.

George Ryland was born in New York around 1830. His father was from Canada, and his mother was from France. George had been in the circus world since at least 1856. That year he was performing with Dan Rice and others in Colonel Joseph Cushing's New York Circus. In May 1857, he broke his shoulder during a fall from his juggling act for the Lee & Bennett's Circus in San Francisco.

George told the story of traveling with his partner and their circus troupe in 1859 to the Sandwich Islands, Honolulu, and Otaheiti (Tahiti.) They played for the kings and queens of these islands, and George was named High Lord Chamberlin and presented with a "wife." The latter was given to a sea captain who took her to Boston and educated her. On the troupe's return, they were shipwrecked off the coast of South America. They were forced to take to the boats reaching Callao, Peru, and then they came back to the States through Mexico.

In the 1860s, George partnered with H. C. Lee in several endeavors in California: The Great Eastern Circus, the Equescurriculum and Camel Show, and the Great New York Circus and Animal Show. In one show, George ascended in his "monster" hot air balloon called Pacific.

In 1870 George lived in San Francisco. Three years later, George, his second wife Ellen, and their animals valued at $60,000 left for tours in Central America. They did very well there. However, while touring in Mexico, "They found the country in a state of rebellion; their horses were confiscated, their elephant, the Prince of Wales, valued at $14,000, killed, and their property generally lost and ruined."

The Rylands were all together in the Phoenix census of 1880. George's oldest son, named George, was born in California in 1851. George's second wife Ellen Jeal (the famous Elena) was born in California in 1852, and their daughter Elena "Nellie" was born in 1875 in Mexico. Nellie was billed as "La Petite Elenata" in a July 1878 performance in Prescott, Arizona. After the Arizona performances from 1878 to 1882, father George was organizing another circus to go back to Mexico.

Daughter "Nellie" became a great equestrienne like her mother. She and her future husband Cecil Lowande starred in Howe's Great London Circus and in Ringling Brothers shows. They married in St. Louis in 1900 and had three sons: Cecil, and twins Herbert and George. Cecil's parents and siblings were also circus performers. Nellie died in 1955 in Petersburg, Illinois.

HOLIDAYS

New Year's celebration à la 1882, published January 2021

According to the *Tombstone Epitaph*, the weather on New Year's Day 1882 was "more like May than January." The newspaper advised their readers, as we do today, that "Now is the accepted time to start in with good resolutions and reformatory pledges . . . The firebell rang its first peal at 12 o'clock this morning in honor of the advent of the new year. There was a general firing of guns and explosion of bombs throughout the town to celebrate the same event."

However, the rival newspaper, the *Tombstone Daily Nugget* reported the heralding event differently. "The dawn of the new year was inaugurated in this city by the brazen tones of the new fire alarm bell, which, for the first time since its acquisition, aroused from peaceful dreams our slumbering inhabitants; and a last tribute of respect was paid to the departed year in volleys fired by the nocturnal portion of our citizens."

New Year's Day was a Sunday, and the Methodist, Episcopal and Catholic churches all held morning services. Several citizens advertised their hours to receive friends. On New Year's Day, Mrs. Chapin and Mrs. Eccleston received from 1 to 9 p.m. On Monday, Mrs. J. A. Kelly, assisted by Mrs. Dr. Ingersoll, received from 2 to 8 p.m.; Mrs. G. G. Berry, assisted by Mrs. Dr. Trenor and newspaperman Mre. C. D. Reppy, 1-9 p.m.; and Mrs. Frank S. Ingoldsby, 12-4 p.m.

Restaurants like the Russ House and the Maison Dore Rotisserie offered delicious entrees, such as: Ham, au Champagne; Chicken Saute with Mushrooms; Fillet of Veal, à la Strasbourgeoise; Venaison (venison), à la Huascar (potato croquettes) and Braized Calf's Tongue with Mushrooms. The next morning, a very novel serenading party was out doing homage to the fair ladies of Tombstone. Three violins, two guitars, two cornets, an alto horn, an organ, and the musicians were all hauled in a large wagon. "The music was considered very fine and no shot-guns were encountered."

Everyone Loves a Parade

The Tombstone Brass Band led the parade from the firehouse on Toughnut Street. Next came Engine Co. 1 with its decorated engine and its mascots "mose" and "lize" who were played by 12-year-old Miss Lottie Moses and Master Norman Woods. The Rescue Hose & Ladder Company came next. Its truck was "tastefully adorned and carrying the Goddess of Liberty" played by Miss Nellie Rafferty. The overhead canopy was ornamented with stars and stripes. Edward Peacock had just repainted the engine after losing a bet on the recent election of a new fire chief. At the end of the parade, the firemen visited each other's firehouses. They next housed the engine, which took place in the engine house, and invitees celebrated with "an ample spread of eatables and drinkables."

That evening the Rescue Hook & Ladder No. 1 hosted the New Year's Ball at Schieffelin Hall. Tickets admitting gentlemen and ladies were $2. Many of the prominent townspeople were on the committees, such as gunsmith G. Spangenberg, saloonkeepers Milt Joyce and "Buckskin Frank" Leslie, pool hall owners Hatch and Campbell, lawmen Johnny Behan and Billy Breakenridge, newspaperman C. D. Reppy, and undertaker Andrew Jackson Ritter. "Great taste was shown in decorating the hall, festooning streamers, banners, emblems, and appropriate mottoes … Dancing was kept up to excellent music until the "wee, sma' hours" were well advanced." Music was provided by Kellogg's band.

RECAPITULATION.	
Tombstone M. & M. Co.	$2,704,936 33
Western (Contention)	2,708,144 39
Grand Central	1,050,875 80
Vizina	526,716 98
Head Center	191,520 52
Boston Mill	112,724 29
Corbin Mill	40,000 00
Ingersoll	15,000 00
Sunset	15,000 00
Total	$7,359,917 81
DIVIDENDS.	
Tombstone M. & M. Co	$1,100,000 00
Western (Contention)	1,375,000 00
Grand Central—Repayment	300,000 00
Grand Central—Dividends	300,000 00
Vizina	60,000 00
Total	$8,135,000 00

Tombstone mines and town businesses were prospering. The *Tombstone Epitaph* reported the record revenue and dividends for the local mines since June 1879 with November and December 1881 numbers approximated.

However, not all was quiet in Tombstone and Pima County. Wyatt Earp's brother Virgil was on the New Year's Ball Reception Committee but was unable to attend the ball due to being ambushed the evening of December 28. On New Year's Eve, about 15 miles from Tombstone, thieves stole horses from Helms' Ranch. And, recently in Dos Cabezos, cattle thieves were at work. A $500 Reward for the thieves was published in the newspaper – "for the apprehension of, and evidence that will convict anyone stealing cattle, horses or mules of the undersigned. Butchers are warned against purchasing stock of our brand from any one but ourselves. Theo F. White & Bros., El Dorado Ranch, Dos Cabezos, P. C., A. T."

Tombstone 1882 celebrated the new year much like we do today. However, its fire alarm bell has been replaced by the glittering ball drop in New York City . . . its actual gunshots replaced by fireworks . . . and its fire department parade replaced by the Tournament of Roses parade (to be reimagined in 2021.) New Year resolutions still abound then and now – and perhaps, some are even kept!

NOTE: The parade paragraph is from my article in the April 2020 *Tombstone Times*.

Love in Tombstone, published February 2021

The biggest holiday in February is, of course, Valentine's Day – the Day of Love. Today, we celebrate with red roses, candy hearts with funny sayings, and perhaps, a marriage proposal!

Although no fancy ads for flowers, candy or jewelry adorned the newspapers in Tombstone on Valentine's Day 1882, the *Nugget* did include the following:

"This is Valentine's day – not sacred to the "Maker," for each of the 364 are to him Valentine day, but sacred from time immemorial to the ardent, but honest and bashful youth, "who fears his fate too much," or the old man's bull dog, and awaits until the 14th of February to tell his love in verse or prose, with a one-cent postage stamp."

It's a little more expensive these days for a verse of love (from Hallmark) and a 55-cent stamp, and the average wedding now costs about $34,000. Tombstone did have its marriages with many of them performed by the local justice of the peace, and anniversaries were a cause for celebration.

On February 12, 1882, just two days before Valentine's Day, John Lawrence and Christine Friel were married by Justice of the Peace A. O. Wallace. No mention, however, was made of bridesmaids, string quartets, tuxedos or a $60/plate reception.

On August 14, 1881, Lois Brown married Spencer Wheeler Clawson. Spencer was a deputy sheriff and later an assistant foreman of the Contention Mine. They later moved to Bisbee, and their Clawson House was built in 1895. It is available for rent even today.

On January 20, 1882, the Charles Glovers celebrated their one-year anniversary. The *Tombstone Epitaph* called it "perhaps the most successful social event which ever took place in Tombstone." The presents were "appropriate and unique, being entirely composed of cotton. The wedding ceremony was performed by the Rev. Fred Brooks . . . Mrs. Glover was attired in a court train of crimson ombré satin, with an overdress of brocaded cream-colored satin. Dancing commenced until 11 o'clock when "an elegant collation was heartily enjoyed." Charles owned a large mercantile store in Tombstone.

However, some love affairs, unfortunately, didn't end too well.

Mike Killeen was 32, a married saloonkeeper from Illinois, but his wife May was not living with him. She was a maid at the Cosmopolitan Hotel. "Buckskin Frank" Leslie (see picture) escorted May home from a local dance on June 22, 1880, and sat with her on the hotel's balcony. Mike was spotted sneaking around the hotel, and when he found Frank and May together, shots were fired. Mike died five days later still swearing revenge on Frank. Frank married the widow on August 5, but they divorced seven years later. Frank then lived with Mollie Edwards and returning home one night caught her speaking to James Neil. Frank shot Mollie to death, and Neil escaped wounded. Frank was sent to Yuma Territorial Prison but was pardoned through the efforts of a divorcee Belle Stowell. Frank married Belle but ran off four months later. Their marriage ended in divorce in 1903.

William "Billy" Kinsman was a 28-year-old miner who was also known as a "sporting man," (i.e. gambler.) He lived with Mrs. May Woodman, aka Road Runner. On December 22, 1881, the *Tombstone Epitaph* printed a marriage notice for Billy and "May Holzerman." (Holds her man??!!) A few days later, a retraction was printed. It said: "Some unprincipled person came into this office a few days ago and required us to publish the announcement of a marriage between Wm. Kinsman and May Holzerman, which we did. It has since been discovered that no such occurrence ever took place, the alleged bridegroom denouncing the statement as an unmitigated falsehood." However, Billy's sister Nellie did marry William Stevens on December 24, and their sister Lottie Kinsman was a witness.

A little over a year later, on February 23, 1883, May was arguing with Billy in front of the Oriental when she shot him. He walked away, and she tried to shoot at him again. May said Billy was abusive to her, and she miscarried while in jail. Found guilty of manslaughter, she was sentenced to five years in Yuma Territorial Prison. Her response to the judge? "May God curse you forever!" In Yuma's registration book, May was 5' 4.5" tall, fair complexion, gray eyes, brown hair, and her occupation was "Ladying." She was later paroled and moved away into obscurity.

We wish you love this Valentine's Day 2021 – and hope that all your loves are everlasting ones.

Christmas in Tombstone 1880 and 1881, published December 2020

Christmas Day 1880, according to George Whitwell Parsons' diary, was a "Fine day. Grand weather." On Christmas Eve, George was master of ceremonies at the Presbyterian church's affair. "Miss Brown read well. Full house, church tastefully ornamented. Large tree loaded down. I had to say a few words to start the thing – present the presents with a few words and wind up the matter." Two presents were particularly fine – a watch to Mrs. Fickas and a clock to Rev. Woods.

Tombstone had plenty of saloons, restaurants, and a few hotels. Businesses were scarce, so those wanting the perfect present found this ad in the newspaper to be most helpful.

> To the People of Tombstone. The holidays are approaching, and those who wish toys, fancy goods, etc., cannot do better than by sending to F. O. Earl & Co., Tucson. Send a list of your children, their ages, sex, and likes, and what amount you wish to invest, and we will fill the order from our large assortment of toys and fancy goods and forward C.O.D.

Or one could try their luck for "a handsome Christmas gift for your wife, sister or mother-in-law." Mrs. Samantha Fallon, who owned the San Jose House, was raffling off a piano.

Or for jewelry (and if one could read 25 cent words) -- this ad was an eye-catcher.

> Holiday Display. Notable among the preparations being made for the approaching holiday trade, is the elaborate collection of fine jewelry, toilet articles and silverware, just received and on exhibition at H. Schmieding's, 508 Allen street. (see ad) An exquisite toilet set in silver and Bohemian glass, around which cluster elegant hunting case gold watches, fine diamonds and a choice line of ladies' and gents' jewelry is simply immense. Call and see the dazzling display, and make your selections for Christmas gifts. (This guy knew how to word an ad!)
> P. Heitzelman's also had jewelry, but he only ran a small ad.

For me, the best part about Christmas is the holiday meal. Beef, pork, mutton and sausage were sold at the Eagle Market, Tribolet Bros. Proprietors. And fresh pies, cakes and candies, breads and rolls were sold at The City Bakery, O. W. Geisenhofer, proprietor.

Not wanting to cook? Go out for a meal at the Arcade Restaurant, Nellie Cashman's sister, Fanny Cunningham, proprietress; the Cosmopolitan Restaurant which had "The Most Elegantly Furnished Dining Room in the Territory;" or the Melrose Restaurant, Mrs. M. L. Woods, Proprietress, which had "The Largest and Most Elegantly Furnished Dining Hall in the city." (Seems to be a little rivalry going on in the wording of those last two ads!)

The miners probably shopped at Shaffer & Lord's, "The Original Miners and Prospectors Store." It carried groceries, provisions, cigars, and the "Best overalls in the city." Books and stationery (to write the loved ones back home) were bought at The Tombstone News Depot, Herman Philippson, proprietor.

And, of course, liquor of all kinds was readily available as well as cigars, tobacco, and the ever-popular firearm. J. J. McClelland carried wines, whiskies and brandies. The "celebrated tobacco -- Tom, Dick and Harry" was at W. A. Bourland's along with 2,000 lbs. of other leading brands. And guns of all kinds were always bought from the famous gunsmith G. F. Spangenberg & Co.

And what about our friend George Whitwell Parsons? He wrote that Christmas Day 1881 was a "charming one." He received a box of cigars from a friend, and the next day, a pretty alligator skin cigar case and match box from his sister. He remarked: "Just in time for my cigars." That night he dined at the Maison Dore with Judge Smith. They had imported oysters and imported claret and champagne, "but neither of us were in the best of humor and didn't care for expense if an enjoyable repast could be had, and we had it." A circus was held below town until early morning "which

70

seemed to terminate in a free fight. Expected a bullet to come up every minute for a while but was spared."

By 1881, Tombstone had grown by leaps and bounds – including more children, new stores, and Christmas presents and delicacies available locally. Entertainment abounded.

The Daily Epitaph advised: "Eat your turkey, drink your egg-nog, go to church, and be as good and as happy as possible to-day; for, remember, Christmas comes but once a year."

Tombstone had three churches -- Catholic, Methodist and Episcopal -- and all held Christmas services.

On December 24 at Schieffelin Hall, the school children's program consisted of songs and recitations. "Handsome and appropriate presents" were attached to the boughs of two nut-pine trees nearly ten feet tall, and 250 children watched as Santa Claus descended from the heavens between the trees. He wore a robe of fur and a shower of snow which was illumined by a red light from the wings of the theater. The teachers received gold pens as presents, and the principal Mr. Sherman's pen had a pearl handle. (That's a pen, not a gun.)

Mrs. Stewart's store carried "Dolls – Small Dolls, Large Dolls" for the little darlings, and there were plenty of places to try one's luck at winning presents.

Summerfield Bros. offered a Grand Gift Enterprise. A $1 ticket bought a chance to win: lady's and men's clothing, blankets, French corsets, Bear skin or Russia leather satchels, lamps, Seth Thomas alarm clocks, or silver-plated cutlery, cups and pickle dishes. 100 winning prize numbers were published later.

Not to be outdone, "The Boss Furnishing Goods House of Arizona" Glover's held "A Holiday Surprise Sale!" It advertised 180,000 prizes with Prize No. 1: interest in the Contention and Grand Central mines; Prize No. 2: 25 miles of the Southern Pacific Railroad, Prize No. 3: A live pig, now on exhibition in their show window, and Prize No. 4: A Straw Hat.

The ladies of the Episcopal Church put on a benefit fair with music, fancy goods, and refreshments. It concluded with a dance. Raffles were held for a book, "The Heart of the White Mountains," (won by Mrs. Hollenbeck), and a silver pitcher and goblet (won by stable owner J. O. Dunbar.) Mrs. Agnes Dunbar received a silver bead necklace for being voted the "Most Popular Lady in Tombstone."

Even the undertakers Ritter & Ream had gifts for sale. Adept at making wooden coffins, they also made mouldings and picture frames, and carried works of art.

A variety of entertainment was available in December 1881. Nellie Boyd and her troupe returned with her plays. The new Hutchinson Troupe presented a Christmas Evening concert at the Bird Cage Opera House. But sadly, actor and solo piccoloist Harry Lorraine who was ill with a cold died that night. His troupe wrote a card of thanks for Tombstone's donations and said he was a "kind friend and genial gentleman."

On Christmas Day, Madame Du Pree and her son Frank began the walking match. Frank had a record of one mile in 6 minutes and 39 seconds, and two miles in 15 minutes. Three local Tombstone men walked two days each, 157+146+139 for a total of 443 miles. $400 was the stake money. However, it was Madame Du Pree who won the match walking all six days and nights for a total of 454 miles.

A Grand Holiday Ball was held December 26 in Contention, and a Grand Uniform Ball was held in Tombstone on January 2 at Schieffelin Hall hosted by the Rescue Hook & Ladder Co. No. 1.

Now for my favorite part! Christmas dinner could be purchased from J. C. Fitzhenry & Co. Dressed turkeys and chicks hailed from Kansas City; wild game and celery from Los Angeles; choice fresh fish from Chicago; and Booths and Mallory's oysters from Baltimore.

If one was a good shot (and the wife didn't mind waiting) -- Gunsmith G. F. Spangenberg held a turkey and chicken shooting match on Christmas Day on the road below the graveyard.

Eating out instead? Besides their usual first-class bill of fare, Rockaway Restaurant also offered roast turkey and suckling pig, together with all the fresh fish, fruits and other delicacies of the season. The biggest menu of all was available at the Russ House (see ad.) Roast turkey, chicken, veal, short ribs of beef, prime beef, dressed lamb, pork, mutton, and bear. Oh my!

ANIMALS AND OTHER CRITTERS

Animal Critters in Tombstone, published March 2021

In its early days, Tombstone was well-known for its cattle and horses. Cattle were raised by thousands, rustled by the hundreds, and sold to local meat markets, both legally and illegally. Horses were a needed commodity; and those, too, were regularly stolen. Several Tombstoners owned expensive race horses which were run at Doling's fairgrounds just south of town.

Several Tombstoners also owned fighting game roosters. Cockfights were held weekly at Walsh's saloon on Allen Street. Unfortunately, business partners William Bobier and Albert Young disagreed over the outcome one night, and Young shot and killed Bobier on July 16, 1882.

Tombstone's youngsters and "town loafers" were known to tie a tin can to a dog or a mule and then run it through town. Known as "kettling," it managed to amuse some, but in the case of Fourtlouis' dog in August 1880 at Vogan & Flynn's saloon, the dog was "turning over tables, chairs, and upsetting faro banks, dealers and all, and taking in a counter filled with glassware just previous to making a leap for the front windows to get out."

Domestic cats were around, and a Tombstoner reported that when his wife sang, the cats were not only jealous, they were mortified. George Whitwell Parsons had two: mother and son "Crow." In September 1880, he was "incensed at the action of one of our two cats on the roof and blazed away in bed at the spot I supposed the cat to be. The bullet didn't go through the roof, but fell back on the cot and the boys made much sport over it. Must have a good pistol. Might need one badly some night."

Many Tombstone stories exist about native-born critters. In his diary, George Whitwell Parsons often wrote about big rattlesnakes, the bad sting of centipedes, the wicked looking tarantulas with legs 2 ½ inches long, and the poisonous lizard "which can jump like a cat." On July 20, 1880, the *Epitaph* newspaper reported: "We noticed on exhibition at Eaton's drug store yesterday, a huge rattlesnake, captured a few miles below town. For its age, it having eight rattles, it is the largest specimen of the species we ever encountered and is well worthy a visit from the curious." Parsons wrote that one man was "rash enough to touch him."

In addition to centipedes, Parsons also encountered scorpions, spiders, and "horse killers" on July 4, 1880. After reading on his cot, he got up barefoot and saw a large centipede by his feet. "The thing got away from me, but I followed it up, pulling up tent poles, etc., till I found it and killed it. A few minutes later, while stripped outside to bathe, another big fellow came charging down upon me and I cut him in two . . . Thought I'd handle my cork hat gently inside tent before putting it on and found a scorpion in that." Upon shaking blankets, he found spiders, horse killers, etc. "Quite a harvest of blood."

Regarding tarantulas, the newspaper also reported in July: "We noticed a partially inebriated man last evening engaged in the delicate pastime of placing a live tarantula into his mouth and closing the same, for the purpose of getting drinks. He repeated the experiment a number of times, escaping unharmed, instinct probably teaching the reptile that preservation is the first law of nature, and to bite him was certain death."

The poisonous lizard referred to above is the Gila monster. Parsons wrote on April 18, 1881, that Captain Hanson brought in a Gila monster to his house, and it looked "like a young alligator." The next month, the *Epitaph* wrote about another one: "This is a monster as is a monster, and no baby at that, it being probably the largest specimen ever captured in Arizona. It is twenty-seven inches long and weighs thirty-five pounds. It was caught by H. C. Hiatt, on the road between Tombstone and the Grand Central mill, and was purchased by Messrs. Ed Baker and Charles Eastman, who now have it on exhibition at Kelley's Wine House, next door above Grand Hotel, Allen street. Eastern people who have never seen one of these monsters, should not fail to inspect his Aztecship, for they might accidently stumble upon one some find day and get badly frightened except they know what it is. They are beautiful pets, they are."

In June the *Epitaph* wrote: "A good joke is told at the expense of a game in the Oriental. It is said that a countryman walked up to one of the tables, Tuesday evening, and wanted to know if a man could bet anything. He was promptly answered, "Bet all you please; bet any d—d thing you've got." The countryman walked out and returned in a moment and placed upon the table a live Gila monster; whereupon there was a big rush, all hands being only too glad to get away."

Many discussed whether the Gila monster's bite was fatal. Dr. Goodfellow wrote a letter to the editor published in the *Scientific American* journal stating it was not. Paying $5 each for a lizard, he had previously studied them and allowed one to bite himself. He was ill for five days but recovered.

Some of the more interesting critters to visit Tombstone were a red bat, a badger, and a wrestling bear. In July 1881, the *Nugget* newspaper reported that a red bat could be seen at the County jail. Deputy Billy Soule charged 25 cents to see it, and he used the fees to buy tobacco for the prisoners. That same month, the *Nugget* reported a live badger was in town. It was "secured by a chain to one of the posts of the awning" at the Maison Doree restaurant. "There he sat entrenched in a small box, and curious and inquisitive dogs interviewed him at a respectful distance."

John Plesant Gray wrote about the wrestling bear's visit to Tombstone: "One summer evening Allen Street was stirred by the appearance of a Gypsyish-looking man wearing big hoop earrings and leading a huge cinnamon-colored bear by a short chain. In a few minutes these stray visitors absorbed the attention of the whole population of Tombstone, and all other business was definitely at a standstill. The Gypsy man was not there for his health, however, and soon he had the sturdy miners interested by offering to bet five dollars a side, the bear against anyone in a wrestling match – the winner being the one who could lay the other down on the street. At first it looked easy for a husky miner, but when the bear stood on his hind legs his head reached over a foot above the tallest miner, and no man's arms were long enough to encircle His Cinnamon-colored Highness around the middle. One miner after another took this turn, but the bear hardly moved from his tracks, no matter what tactics were used against him. Some thought they could pick up one of the bear's feet and thus throw him off balance, but the monster stood like a statue and no one was able to lift the bear's leg even the least little bit from the ground.

"The bear showed wonderful patience, as if he were sure of his power. After prolonged efforts of an opponent to no avail, his owner would speak one word and Mr. Bear would place his paws around his opponent's body, gently lift the man off the ground, and as gently lay him down in the dust of the street. Nearly every miner wanted a turn at it and the five dollar bills fell on the Gypsy like rain. It was more fun to the crowd than anything that ever happened in Tombstone. Even when it got too dark to continue with the performance, the crowd kept urging the bear's owner to come back the next day for more. But Gypsy and bear disappeared that night for good, and it was rumored that the saloons, gambling joints, and dance halls had bestowed a good-sized purse on the Gypsy in order to get him to beat it out of town with his bear game."

EDUCATION 1881

An 1881 Tombstone primer, published June 2021

Remember the popular game show "Are You Smarter than a 5th Grader?" It showed how much we have forgotten as adults. In 1881 Tombstone, they boasted of the children's schooling and their teachers considering them one of the best in the country. Below is a sample of some of the questions on a test in November. Try your luck at these. Answers below the questions.

Fifth Grade Questions

Arithmetic: How many acres of land in one section, in a quarter section, and what is the smallest legal sub-division recognized by the government? How many sections of land in a township?

Language: Correct the following: When i was a Little Boy i saw a old man Riding toward the citys of new York and Brooklyn. The leafes were falling from the trees by the handsful.

Geography: Bound Massachusetts: give its chief cities, rivers, mountain range and cape; and by whom was it first settled?

Higher Geography: What is the snowline?

Third Grade Questions

Geography: How can you prove the earth is round?

Language: Write all the verbs in the following sentences. Good students study hard. The horse ran down the hill. Dogs bark.

Answers

Arithmetic answer by Georgie Russell: There are 640 acres of land in a section, 160 in a quarter section. The smallest legal sub-division, recognized by the government, is 40 acres. There are 36 sections of land in a township.

Language answer by Selma Fonck (age 12): When I was a little boy, I saw an old man riding toward the cities of New York and Brooklyn. The leaves were falling from the trees by the handfuls.

Geography answer by Lula Colp (age 11): Massachusetts is bounded on the north by Vermont and New Hampshire, east by the Atlantic Ocean, south by Connecticut and Rhode Island, and west by New York. Its cities are Cambridge, Springfield, Lowell, Worcester, Fall River and Boston. The rivers are Connecticut and Maryland; mountain range Green, Cape Cod the cape. It was first visited by Captain John Smith.

Higher Geography answer by Lucy Herrick (age 14): The snow line is the point where there is snow the year around. At the equator its height is about three miles, and at the arctic region, it is at the sea level.

Geography answer by Lizzie Murphy (age 10): We know that the earth is round, because, starting at a given place, and going directly straight, we return to the place we started from.

Language answer by Fannie Healy (age 9) and Albert Wade (age 10): Study, Ran, Bark.

Want a few more?

Here are some questions, but you'll need to confirm your answers! Good luck!

Arithmetic: Bought 5 lbs 8 oz. of opium, at 50 cents an ounce, avoirdupois weight, and sold the same by apothecaries' weight at $10 per pound. What was gained? (Seriously, they asked the children about opium!!)

Language: How do nouns ending in f and fe form their plurals? How do nouns ending in y form their plurals?

Geography: How many degrees are the tropics from the equator? How many degrees is the arctic circle from the North Pole?

FROM *FORGET ME NOT*

My first book was called *Forget Me Not: A Boothill Remembrance*. It highlights the Boothill Cemetery in Tombstone and all those who are probably buried there. The *Tombstone Times* ran my first serial from the book July through December 2019.

Forget Me Not Series – Eulogies - Malcolm Campbell, George E. Whitcher, and Archie McBride, published July 2019

In the rough and tumble Tombstone of the early 1880s, a wisp of literary poignancy ran through the town. Several townspeople displayed this in their published eulogies of three men who died and were buried in Boothill. I was amazed to find such sweet, touching writings in a town known for its cow-boys, gamblers and "soiled doves." Here are the stories and eulogies of Malcolm Campbell, George E. Whitcher, and Archie McBride.

Malcolm Campbell died on March 17, 1882, of pneumonia at the age of 35. He was an unmarried miner and carpenter from Canada and a member of the Knights of Pythias. An anonymous memory article was printed about him in *The Tombstone Epitaph* of March 29, 1882. A Christian in his ways, Malcolm had helped a young mother in distress.

To the Memory of Malcom Campbell.
[Communicated.]

His was a life of purity and truth seldom surpassed. Not all those claiming to be ordained of God have the kindly heart or purity of mind attained by this dead friend. By chance we met, I a homeless wanderer, seeking among strangers with sad and troubled heart, the food and shelter for my orphaned children. Toil seemed heavier in this strange land where none were bound by tie of kindred blood, yet his cheering smile and counsel wise and kind made the weak heart brave. He was a toiler in this human hive. Like him of Bethlehem, a carpenter, and like him meek and lowly yet a godly man; of earth, but not polluted with those earthly sins which are so strong a trait of modern men. One of the few was he who realize that mental power should ever hold in strict abeyance the base physical. No taint of scandal breathed across those lips; no word of blasphemy his tongue would frame; no maddening drinks in him found votary. Of no dishonorble act or base injustice could his great heart be guilty. Yet he was little known and now he lies within a little lonely unmarked grave in a strange land, with few to mourn, gave one greatly indebted to him for sympathy and kindness given disinterestedly as his great heart could give.

"To the Memory of Malcolm Campbell.

His was a life of purity and truth seldom surpassed. Not all those claiming to be ordained of God have the kindly heart of purity of mind attained by this dear friend. By chance we met, I a homeless wanderer, seeking among strangers with sad and troubled heart, the food and shelter for my orphaned children. Toil seemed heavier in this strange land where none were bound by tie of kindred blood, yet his cheering smile and counsel wise and kind made the weak heart brave. He was a toiler in this human hive. Like him of Bethlehem, a carpenter, and like him meek and lowly yet a godly man; of earth, but not polluted with those earthly sins which are so strong a trait of modern men. One of the few he was who realize that mental power should ever hold in strict abeyance the base physical. No taint of scandal breathed across those lips; no word of blasphemy his tongue would frame; no maddening drinks in him found votary. Of no dishonorable act or base injustice could his great heart be guilty. Yet he was little known and now he lies within a little lonely unmarked grave in a strange land, with few to mourn, save one greatly indebted to him for sympathy and kindness given disinterestedly as his great heart could give."

George E. Whitcher was the son of Jeremiah Whitcher, a prominent surveyor and civil engineer who created the official Oakland map in 1860. George was only 22 and a miner at the Russell mine. He was on top of the cage on April 14, 1882. It accidentally released, and he went down the shaft to his death. "F" wrote the following eulogy for George in *The Tombstone Epitaph* of April 18, 1882.

"Again the mysterious "shadow fear'd of man" has thrown its dark, chill mantle o'er the form of one our hearts loved well. Summoned in one brief moment to stand before his Maker, dear George has gone, and left us mourning by the senseless grave – mourning as memory's light reveals the manliness, honor and fidelity now fled with Death – mourning in sympathy with his grief-burdened and sorrowing family.

"Brave, filled with energetic life, anxious to be leading, he stepped upon his fatal threshold, and the door was held ajar. Another instant, and he was hurled head-foremost down the frightful corridor of gloom, to find a resting place upon the cruel rocks that lapped his young life's ebbing flow.

"Quickly but tenderly they bore him from that bed of horror to the bright glow of day, but Hope had winged her flight. One, two, three, the hours dragged on; the tired minutes were slowly following, when Lo! he opened wide his eyes, as though to bid farewell to Earth, and left us.

"A mist dimmed the stars." F.

Archie McBride was a well-known sportsman and hotelkeeper of the Grand Hotel in Tombstone. He died of consumption on May 14, 1882. In late 1881, he and his wife Frances had refurnished the hotel in an elegant style. New ash furniture came from St. Louis. The club room had rich wallpaper, a Brussels carpet, and deep flowing lace drapery. Frances selected window plants for each bedroom, and ivies and climbers graced the second-floor porch. The Grand Hotel was the favorite hotel of Ike and Phin Clanton and Johnny Ringo. Archie's eulogy was written by Colonel Charles D. Poston in *The Tombstone Epitaph* of May 20, 1882. Colonel Poston was a U.S. Congressman, a Superintendent of Indian Affairs, a lawyer and an explorer.

The Memory of the Dead.

Colonel Charles D. Poston, one of the keenest of observers and most genial of men, puts the following flower on the grave of Archie McBride:

"Archie McBride has, in the vernacular of the country, handed in his checks, and we may hope they will be redeemed by the great Banker of Calvary, whose treasury of mercy is never exhausted.

"The trotting park at Lansingburg and the course of Saratoga will grieve at the departure of one of the gentlest spirits that ever graced the turf or crossed the green fields of sport.

"McBride was well known on the Pacific coast and especially in Prescott, Tucson and Tombstone. If gentle manners constitute a gentleman, he was a prince of the green cloth, or the cloth of gold. A year ago he was married to Miss Sheriff of Prescott, by the Rev. Dr. Gregory, pastor of the First Baptist church of Tucson, and died in the bonds of holy wedlock.

"A keen sportsman, a generous friend and a boon companion, he has gone where 'Roger and I will require neither victuals nor drink;' and as he was wont to do in this world, let us 'welcome the coming and speed the parting guest.'

"Archie was proprietor of the Grand Hotel at Tombstone, when he died and was surrounded by all the comforts which an affectionate wife and devoted friends could supply; but tubercular consumption had fastened on his lungs and the ignorance of medical science was not able to eliminate the seeds of disease from his lungs. No man should be allowed to die under a hundred years and the doctors are responsible for premature deaths. Their errors of living men are exposed to his public gaze. As Socrates said to his friends when he was preparing the ferriage for Charon, 'The immortal Gods only know, my friends, who shall be happier to-morrow, you or I.'

"The genial spirit has passed to realms unknown, where we may hope evolution continues its expansion and development."

"Colonel Charles D. Poston, one of the keenest of observers and most genial of men, puts the following flower on the grace of Archie McBride:

"Archie McBride has, in the vernacular of the country, handed in his checks, and we may hope they will be redeemed by the great Banker of Calvary, whose treasury of mercy is never exhausted.

"The trotting park at Lansingburg and the course of Saratoga will grieve at the departure of one of the gentlest spirits that ever graced the turf or crossed the green fields of sport.

"McBride was well known on the Pacific coast and especially in Prescott, Tucson and Tombstone. If gentle manners constitute a gentleman, he was a prince of the green cloth, or the cloth of gold. A year ago he was married to Miss Sheriff of Prescott, by the Rev. Dr. Gregory, pastor of the First Baptist church of Tucson, and died in the bonds of holy wedlock.

"A keen sportsman, a generous friend and a boon companion, he has gone where 'Roger and I will require neither victuals nor drink;' and as he was wont to do in this world, let us 'welcome the coming and speed the parting guest.'

"Archie was proprietor of the Grand Hotel at Tombstone, when he died and was surrounded by all the comforts which an affectionate wife and devoted friends could supply; but tubercular consumption had fastened on his lungs and the ignorance of medical science was not able to eliminate the seeds of

disease from his lungs. No man should be allowed to die under a hundred years and the doctors are responsible for premature deaths. Their mistakes are buried in the grave, but the errors of living men are exposed to the public gaze. As Socrates said to his friends when he was preparing the ferriage for Charon, 'The immortal Gods only know, my friends, who shall be happier tomorrow, you or I.'

"The genial spirit has passed to realms unknown, where we may hope evolution continues its expansion and development."

Forget Me Not Series - Red Light, published August 2019

"Queen of the Red Light District" – Dutch Annie, Big Nose Maggie, and fortune tellers Madame Louise Neilson and Madame Ralph

What would old Tombstone be like without its "madams," "soiled doves," and fortune tellers. Fortune tellers? Yes, fortune tellers. Madame Louise Neilson and Madame Ralph both wielded their trade in Tombstone in the early 1880s. The "Queen of the Red Light District" was, of course, the beloved Dutch Annie. She was probably the best-known madam of all and was buried in Boothill. But did you know that another madam named Big Nose Maggie was also buried in Boothill? Men with lots of money loved spending it on their "entertainment," and these women were happy to provide it … for a price!

Madame Louise Neilson was an English lady who died of a lung abscess about October 14, 1883. She was divorced from William Neilson. Madame Louise had been telling fortunes for some time in Tombstone. At the time of her death, William was representing Sarah Althea "Allie" Hill in her scandalous divorce case against former Senator William Sharon from

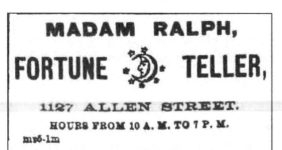

Nevada. William came to Tombstone to identify Louise's body, and she was buried in Boothill. Although no ad was found in the newspaper for her, there was one for **Madame Ralph** in March 1882 issues of *The Tombstone Epitaph*. In the June 3rd issue, the newspaper reported that Prescott had a fortune teller, too.

According to Boothill records, **Dutch Annie**, sometimes called the Queen of the Red Light District, died in 1883. Dutch Annie was issued a business license in 1881 for a "house of ill fame." One author wrote that she was arrested in Tombstone with Augustine Martinez for using indecent language. Another author wrote that she was "distinguished by great kindness of heart and many charities," and thousands of carriages were at her funeral. Dutch Annie was definitely a mixture of roughness and kindness. In January 1938 at Quong Gu/Gee Kee's funeral, Mike Coffee remembered both Dutch Annie and Big Nosed Maggie were buried in Boothill. In an interview published in *The Arizona Daily Star* on January 16, he said that although Dutch Annie had no social standing, she "took care of more charities in her time than lots of the pillars of the church." However, ten years after her death, *The Tombstone Epitaph* of April 5, 1893, reported that Dutch Annie was a "landmark" who had left Tombstone for New York and Boston after she sold her Sixth Street house twice – conditionally on her death, but she wasn't, and unconditionally to another party which the court allowed. Perhaps, this was a different Dutch Annie?

> **Annie's Antics.**
>
> Another landmark has gone from Tombstone. "Dutch Annie" has left for New York. She made her last appearance before Justice Duncan yesterday afternoon in a case wherein Miles Gibbons and Dr. Wright were plaintiffs. She made a conditional bill of sale to them for debts due, of her house on 6th street in Tombstone. The conditions were that the sale should go into effect if she died. She made an unconditional sale of the same property yesterday to E. Lenormand of this city. Mr. Gibbons caused her arrest for felony.
>
> Justice Duncan looked into the matter, noted the conditions of the first sale, took a good look at her to be sure she wasn't dead, and declared that she was not guilty.
>
> She tripped out of the front door like a girl of sixteen and in one hour afterward was on her way to New York by private conveyance via Benson.

Big Nosed Maggie's death date is unknown. As stated above, Mike Coffee remembered both Dutch Annie and Big Nosed Maggie being buried in Boothill. He said that although she had no social standing, Maggie was always caring for someone in trouble. When she died, "they closed up the town, hung crepe on the doors and everybody and his brother went to the burying."

All these women earned their place in Tombstone. Although by society standards, they were shunned by the "good" women and men. Yet, stories of their kindness and charity live on in the Old West newspapers.

Forget Me Not Series – Gamblers, published September 2019

Gambling in old Tombstone ranked right up there with drinking and prostitution. It was reported that over $10 million changed hands in the eight-year long poker game in the basement of the Bird Cage Theatre. Faro was a popular game, too. James Earp, Wyatt's brother, dealt faro as did Morgan at the Oriental Saloon.

Thomas C. Bridge died on September 8, 1879. Both Tucson's *Arizona Citizen* and Prescott's *The Weekly Arizona Miner* newspapers reported the death on September 12. Thomas was stabbed by Brocky Smith on August 10 while playing a game of cards at Clark & Miffin's saloon in Tombstone. Brocky went to Charleston, was arrested, escaped to the Huachucas, and no one went after him.

Charley Storms died on February 25, 1881. The Tucson and Sacramento newspapers carried the story of Charley's death from a gunshot wound. Sacramento said: The cause leading to the shooting was reported to have been a "gambling transaction." Charley was killed by Luke Short who was dealing faro at the Oriental. According to one report, Charley called him out, and let Luke fire first. Another report said Luke hid and fired at Charley.

George Whitwell Parsons wrote in his journal that he went outside on hearing the third shot and saw Charley die in the street – "shot in the heart." Luke's case was dismissed on June 4, 1881. Born in 1821, Charley went to California in '49. He was a well-known sportsman in Pioche, Virginia City, Deadwood, Leadville, and other mining camps.

Boothill records state that a **Thomas Morgan** died in 1882. This could have been Morgan, the gambler. The *Tombstone Daily Nugget* newspaper of March 5 and Tucson's *Arizona Weekly Citizen* of March 12 reported Morgan was riding in the stagecoach from Tombstone to Charleston on March 4. He was fashioning a pillow out of his overcoat, when his pistol dropped hitting the floor. It discharged and shot him in the right side. He only lived 30 minutes and said nothing. However, the newspapers did not record his first name.

Boothill records state that a **Jack King** was buried there. Although no record of him was found from 1879 to 1883, there was a Phoenix gambler named Jack King in 1909. According to the *Bisbee Daily Review* on October 7, Jack was visiting in Bisbee when he decided to elope with John Dye's wife Althea, age 45, and daughter Lillian, age 17. Jack was later arrested and sentenced in Courtland, 15 miles northeast of Tombstone. He was fined $300 and six months in jail. This Jack gambled a lot … and lost.

Miners who risked their lives daily in the silver mines

"Hat's Off" to the hard-working Tombstone miners of the 1880s. Many miners came from the California, Nevada and northern Arizona Territory mine camps. Many left their families behind or placed them with relatives in more civilized towns. Many miners came from Ireland and Germany. One ship's manifest page in 1875 listed 55 passengers from England and Ireland, and 16 of them were miners.

Miners risked their lives every day to go down into the deep shafts. Mine accidents in Tombstone were usually caused by human error, and they usually involved the mine shaft and the cages. The following are nine miners' stories in chronological order for the years 1879 through 1883. They are all buried in Boothill. Several miners were killed when they fell to the bottom of the shaft. One was overcome by fumes after going into the shaft too soon after setting off an explosive. One was a carpenter who fell off a gallows frame. These men formed a brotherhood of sorts, and their funerals were largely attended by their fellow miners.

Samuel Brown died on August 22, 1879. Samuel, age 23, was a mineworker in the Carbonate mine in the Tombstone Mining District. Major Thomas Morgan relayed the information to Tucson's *Arizona Citizen* newspaper. The article said he was "a clever and energetic young man, liked and respected by all who knew him." One day he shot off several blasts at the bottom of a shaft. He went into the shaft too soon. He was overcome by smoke and fell to the bottom. A fellow worker tried to rescue him, but the smoke was too thick. Finally, Superintendent Meade brought the body out. Samuel came from Pennsylvania, and his father was the foreman of the Cambria Iron Works in Johnstown.

Patrick Conners died on April 11, 1881. Patrick and his Empire Mine co-worker C. Sullivan were at the 452' level of the mine. Patrick and Sullivan had just loaded their shots. Patrick got into the bucket. Sullivan placed the lit snuffs and got in the bucket, and they rang to hoist it. Nothing happened, so they rang again. Patrick stepped out just as the bucket rose. He grabbed onto the bucket rim and held on. But before reaching the top, he lost his grasp and fell 375 feet to his death. He was 28 years old and a member of the Knights of Pythias.

J. D. Dernitt/Demitt was only 23 years old when he fell 368' into the Head Center mine shaft. J. D. had brought in his car of ore but rang the wrong bell. He tried to correct his error, but he fell. Hugh McDermott was working at the 500' level and heard him fall. The local newspapers reported that he was a steady, industrious carman, and the coroner jury ruled accidental death – probably sudden vertigo. He died on June 8, 1881. J.D. was from Illinois.

James Tulley died on October 5, 1881. James was 37, a carpenter and miner for the Grand Central Mine. He previously had worked at Gold Hill, California. James was working on a platform 20' below the surface. Engineer Stevens hoisted him up but mistakenly let the hoist go to the top – 45' above ground. The cart tipped over, and James fell 125 feet to his death. Engineer Stevens was overwhelmed with grief, and the mine closed for the funeral. The Tombstone brass band was at the head of the procession followed by about 200 miners. The *Tombstone Daily Nugget* newspaper wrote about the impressive funeral saying: "...not from the number who followed the unfortunate victim ... but those who followed through the mud were hardy miners, men who day after day take their lives in their hands when they descend into the depths of the earth, not knowing what may happen e'er their labor is finished." James' brother Peter did file a wrongful death suit against the Grand Central Mining Company for $50,000. The other two brothers were Patrick and John.

George Whitcher died on April 14, 1882. George was 22 and a miner at the Russell mine, and he and another man were on top of the cage. When the cage was released, it jerked and went down. One man jumped off, but George went down the shaft with the cage to his death. His brother John worked at a nearby mine, and their father Jeremiah lived in Tombstone for several years. In 1880 Jeremiah confirmed the water company's sources to supply at least 10,000 Tombstone residents, and he was a candidate for Town Engineer.

John Plate died on May 17, 1882. A few days before his death, John, age 40 from Germany, had arrived in Tombstone. He missed getting into the cage at the Grand Central Mine and fell 200' to his death. John had lost an eye in a January explosion at the Mono tunnel in Pioche, Nevada. Perhaps, this condition contributed to his death. He was survived by his wife Mary and their three children: Susie, age 6, Della, age 4, and Harry, age 2.

Michael Hoarty died on May 15, 1883. He and William Ross, age 24 from California, were in the cage at the Head Center mine, and it stopped short of the level. Michael put his foot out on a bar, and when the cage rose, he was trapped for a second between the cage and the timbers.

William immediately rang the bell, and the cage stopped. Four days after his injury, Michael died from peritonitis. He was age 31 from Ireland, and he had lived in Charleston since 1880.

William Brokaw died on July 1, 1883. About 32 years old, William fell 30 feet from a ladder in the pump shaft at the Contention Mine. He struck the floor on the 300' level and died just moments after Dr. George Goodfellow arrived. Examination of the body revealed no external injuries, so it was unclear if death was caused by the fall or some internal problem.

Matthew Harris was 28 years old and a carpenter at the Contention Mine. He was a native of Nova Scotia who had been in Tombstone since 1881. Matthew was at the Flora Morrison Hoist works for only a few days when he accidentally fell 24' off the gallows frame to his death. He died on July 22, 1883.

Forget Me Not Series – Statistics, published November 2019

The Boothill cemetery was open from 1878 through 1883 and over 300 citizens were buried there. Diseases or natural causes took the most lives – about 85 – and over 60 deaths were from unknown causes. The most famous, of course, were those killed by gunshots – Old Man Clanton, Billy Clanton, Frank and Tom McLaury, William "Billy the Kid" Claiborne, Charley Storms, John Hicks, Mike Killeen, Tom Waters (killed for the color of his shirt,) Marshal Fred White, James Hickey, Martin Peel, and William Grounds.

The Tombstone Epitaph on January 1, 1882, published Ritter & Ream Undertakers' statistics of 55 deaths between March 1 and December 31, 1881. The headline read: "The Garnerings of the Rider of the Pale Horse Whose Name is Death." Surprisingly, Tombstone's death rate was 9.5 per thousand, whereas San Francisco's was 11. Tombstone deaths included: "pneumonia 8, mania a potu 2, heart disease 4, shot and robbed 1, falling down mining shaft 3, gunshot wounds 5, congestion of brain 1, congestion of stomach 1, Bright's disease of the kidneys 1, small pox 1, run over by wagons 2, suicides 5, congestion of the lungs 2, inflammation of the bowels 1, typhoid malaria fever 1, child birth 2, unknown cause 4, general debility 1, blood poison 1, consumption 1. Causes of the deaths of children: whooping cough, gastric fever, etc."

Children's deaths are always the saddest. Several children were stillborn or died as infants. Hilly Hickson was 9 when he died a few days after falling from his stilts, and James "Joe" Sowle was 14 when he died from a lightning strike. Dr. George Goodfellow, the famous Tombstone doctor, lost his little son on July 18, 1882. George Jr., was only 8 weeks old and died from intestinal hemorrhaging. Dr. Goodfellow had saved so many Tombstone lives, but he could not save his little son.

The deaths are categorized in the book, *Forget Me Not*. The results are shown in the table.

Life in Tombstone in the 1880s was a gamble because of so many factors: epidemic diseases, limited medical knowledge, dangerous occupations, chronic drinking, the criminal element, and a quickly growing population. The national average life span was about 40 years, and those who attained 50 in the West were called "Old Timers." Many citizens gave their lives to birth "The Town Too Tough to Die." May they "Rest in Peace."

Tombstone's Boothill

Natural causes – 41 with 44 more described specifically as:
pneumonia 14, heart disease 7, typhoid 5, consumption 4,
diphtheria 3, and one each for brain fever, bronchopneumonia,
cancer surgery, fever, food poisoning, leprosy unconfirmed,
measles, meningitis, scarlet fever unconfirmed, nephritis, and
old age.

Unknown – 61

Gunshot – 57 with 13 unconfirmed

Accident – 25 with one unconfirmed

Mine accident – 10

Suicide – 10 with 2 unconfirmed

Legal hanging – 8

Overdose – 6

Childbirth – 5 with 1 unconfirmed

Killed by Apaches – 5 with 1 unconfirmed

Stabbed – 5 with 2 unconfirmed

Killed by Indians – 4 with 2 unconfirmed

Beaten/blow or accident/blow to the head – 3

Drowned – 3

Lynched – 3 with 2 unconfirmed

Alcoholism – 1

Blood poisoning – 1

Hog bite – 1

Lightning – 1

Malnourished – 1

Opium poisoning – 1

Stoned – 1

Unconfirmed – 1 killed in a stampede, 3 killed, and 3 murdered

Two racehorse owners are buried in Boothill: James Halstead and Archie McBride

In March 1880, John Doling conceived the idea of a race track near Tombstone, and on May 7, the races began. Conveyance fare to the race was 50 cents. The first day was a quarter mile dash between Tom Gardner's "Dolly" and J. R. Simmons' bay mare "Molly S" for a prize of $1,000. Races were held on the next two days as well: a dash of 600 yards and a handicap race, free for all. Horse racing was very popular in the mining camps of the West, and the 6th running of the Kentucky Derby was held on May 18 at Churchill Downs.

Englishman **James Halstead** owned an expensive trotting horse called Pluck. He came to Tombstone in April 1880 and was staying at the Mohave Hotel. Presumably, he came to Tombstone to race his horse. Unfortunately, James died about June 9, 1880, at the age of 43, and was buried in Boothill. Pluck was then sold to M. Lazard for $300.

However, the year before, James' horse Pluck and **Archie McBride**'s racer Vaughn went head-to-head in two races. From Ireland, Archie McBride was a well-known sportsman in California, and in 1877, he was part owner of the Cabinet Saloon in Prescott.

On October 19, 1879, Pluck raced Vaughn in Prescott's Whipple Park. Vaughn won the first and third heats and the money; Pluck won the second heat. However, on December 12, Pluck evened the score in a trotting race – one mile and repeat – at Lee and Gardner's track south of Tucson. Pluck won the first heat in 2:53 ½, was second in the second heat to Vaughn, and won the third heat, race, and money in 3:10.

Archie later opened club rooms in Tucson and then came to Tombstone in January 1882. He and his wife leased the Grand Hotel, and they refurnished it in an elegant style. The Grand Hotel was the favorite hotel of Ike and Phin Clanton and Johnny Ringo. Unfortunately, Archie had consumption, and he died in Tombstone on May 14, 1882. He was also buried in Boothill.

Tombstone's Driving Park held horse races for many years. On Christmas Day 1880, the first race was a trotting race, mile and repeat, for a prize of $100. Entries were: Virgil Earp's "Old Doc," Wyatt Earp's "Sorrel Reuben," and James Vogan's "Prince." James Vogan was a miner and a saloonkeeper. The second race, a single dash of a mile for $50, listed two entries: Smith Gray's "Sorrel Frank" and Mark Shaffer's grey mare. Smith Gray was a liveryman, and Mark Shaffer was a Tombstone merchant. On July 3, 1882, J. O. Dunbar's horse "Comanche Joe" beat F. B. Boarman's horse "Prince." Winning time was 52 seconds. J. O. Dunbar was a liveryman, newspaperman, and a county treasurer. F. B. (Frank Brent) Boarman was a Tombstone merchant.

Tombstone Driving Park was located a mile from town. It not only held horse races, but it was also used by the baseball team, for boxing and wrestling matches, and for community events.

BIBLIOGRAPHY

Primary Sources
Cochise County Coroner's Inquests
Great Registers – voting registers
Minutes Books, A-E, Common Council, Village of Tombstone

Government Sources
Military Records and/or Pension files, National Archives
   and Records Services
United States Census

Newspapers
Bisbee *Arizona Daily Orb*
Bisbee Daily Review
Daily Tombstone
Flagstaff *Arizona Champion*
Fort Worth Daily Gazette
Globe *Arizona Silver Belt*
Daily Los Angeles Herald
Mesilla Valley Independent
Oasis from Arizola
Phoenix Herald
Prescott *Weekly Arizona Miner*
Sacramento Daily Record-Union
Safford *Graham Guardian*
St. John's Herald
The Washington Post
Tombstone Epitaph
Tombstone Nugget
Tombstone Prospector
Tombstone Times
Tucson *Arizona Citizen*
Tucson *Arizona Daily Star*
Tucson *Arizona Weekly Citizen*
Tucson *El Fronterizo*
Tucson *Weekly Arizona Citizen*
Yuma *Arizona Sentinel*

Books and Booklets

Ackerman, Rita. *Tombstone: Who, What, When, Where.* Privately published, 2005.

Aros, Joyce. *The Cochise County Cowboys: Who were these men?* Tombstone: Goose Flats Publishing, 2011.

Bailey, Lynn R. *Too Tough to Die: The Rise, Fall, and Resurrection of a Silver Camp; 1878 to 1990.* Tucson: Westernlore Press, 2004.

Boothill Graveyard: A Descriptive List of the more than 250 Graves in Boothill. Tombstone, privately published.

Breakenridge, William M. *Helldorado: Bringing the Law to the Mesquite.* Boston: Houghton Mifflin Company, 1928.

Bret Harte, John. *The San Carlos Indian Reservation 1872-1886: An Administrative History.* Tucson, AZ: The University of Arizona, 1972.

Burns, Walter Noble. *Tombstone: An Iliad of the Southwest.* Garden City, N.Y: Doubleday, Page & Company, 1927.

Disturnell, W. C. *Arizona Business Directory and Gazetteer 1881.* San Francisco: Bacon & Co. Printers, 1881. Located on Azmemory.azlibrary.com, under PUBLICATIONS

Eppinga, Jane. *Around Tombstone: Ghost Towns and Gunfights*. Charleston, S.C.: Arcadia Publishing, 2009.

-------. *Tombstone.* Charleston, S.C.: Arcadia Publishing, 2003.

Gray, John Plesent. *Tombstone's Violent Years, 1880-1882*. Tucson: Trail to Yesterday Books, 1999.

-------. *When All Roads Led to Tombstone*. Boise, ID: Tamarack Books, Inc., 1998.

Lake, Carolyn, editor, *Under Cover for Wells Fargo: The Unvarnished Recollections of Fred Dodge*. Norman, Oklahoma: University of Oklahoma Press, 1969, renewed 1997.

McCool, Grace. *Gunsmoke: The True Story of Old Tombstone*. Tucson: Treasure Chest Publications, Inc.,1990. Reprint of Bakarich, Sarah Grace, 1954.

-------. *So Said the Coroner*. Tombstone, AZ: The Tombstone Epitaph, 1968.

Nunnelley, Lela. *Boothill Grave Yard*. Tombstone: privately published, 1962.

Parsons, George W. *The Private Journal of George Whitwell Parsons*. Phoenix: Arizona Statewide Archival and Records Project, September 1939. Also printed as *A Tenderfoot in Tombstone*, edited by Lynn R. Bailey. Tucson, AZ: Westernlore Press, 1996.

-------. *The Private Journal of George Whitwell Parsons, Volume Two,* edited by Carl Chafin. Tombstone, AZ: Cochise Classics, 1997.

Shillingberg, William B. *Tombstone, A.T.: A History of Early Mining, Milling, and Mayhem*. Norman: University of Oklahoma Press, 1999.

Sonnichsen, C. L. *Billy King's Tombstone: The Private Life of an Arizona Boomtown*. Caldwell, Idaho: The Caxton Printers, Ltd., 1942.

State of Arizona. *Arizona Death Records*. Tucson, AZ: State of Arizona, 1976.

Traywick, Mary D. and Ben T. *Tombstone's Other Cemetery*. Tombstone, AZ: Privately published, 2005.

Traywick, Ben T. *Tombstone's Boothill*. Tombstone, AZ: Red Marie's Bookstore, 1994.

-------. *Death's Doings in Tombstone*. Tombstone, AZ: Red Marie's Books, 2002.

-------. *The Residents of Tombstone's Boothill*. Tombstone, AZ: privately published, 1971.

-------. *Tombstone's Clippings*. Tombstone, AZ: Red Marie's Books, 1989, 1994.

Tucson and Tombstone General and Business Directory, for 1883 and 1884. Tucson: Cobler & Co., 1883.

Underhill, Lonnie. *Biographical Dictionary, 1880*. Gilbert, AZ: Roan Horse Press, 2011.

-------. *Biographical Dictionary, 1881*. Gilbert, AZ: Roan Horse Press, 2013.

-------. *Index to Daily Nugget, Volume 1, 1880*. Gilbert, AZ: Roan Horse Press, 2011.

-------. *Index to Tombstone Epitaph, 1880, 1881 (2 volumes) and 1882.* Gilbert, AZ: Roan Horse Press, 2010.

Waters, Frank. *The Earp Brothers of Tombstone: The Story of Mrs. Virgil Earp.* New York: Clarkson N. Potter Inc., 1960. Reprint Lincoln, NE: University of Nebraska Press, 1976. [Original manuscript entitled *Tombstone Travesty.*]

Internet websites

Arizona Death Certificates at genealogy.az.gov/
Arizona Memory Project – Cochise County Territorial Documents, newspapers, oral histories, people, photographs, and publications at azmemory.azlibrary.gov/digital/
Arizona State Archives available on Ancestry.com
Bisbee, Arizona at www.discoverbisbee.com
Chronicling America – newspapers at chroniclingamerica.loc.gov/
Ellis Island records at www.myheritage.com
Familysearch.org – National census and military records (made available by LDS)
Findagrave.com
Library of Congress at www.loc.gov/
Newspapers.com
Online encyclopedia at www.wikipedia.org
Tombstone Boothill Gift Shop at tombstoneboothillgiftshop.com
Yuma Territorial Prison at corrections.az.gov/adc-history

INDEX

Residents of Tombstone
*denotes non-resident

Clum, John 23-24, 58
Cockburn, Carlotta "Lottie" 18
Coffee, Mike 83
Collins, Horatio 39
Colp, Lula 78
Conners, Patrick 85
Contreras, Maria 49
Cook, Mr. 39
Corrigan, Thomas 50
Cosper, A. A. 20
Cowing, Rufus 50
*Crabtree, Charlotte "Lottie" 18, 36
Crabtree, John Ashworth Jr. 18
Crane, Jim 11
Crumblish, Maggie 24
Cunningham, Fanny 70
*Davenport, Mr. 43
De Wees, J. H. 37
Dean, E. H. 48
Deger, Lawrence 15
Dernitt/Demitt, J. D. 86
Dickerson, E. 37
Diehl, Pony 13
Dodge, Fred 7, 10
Doling, John 90
*Du Pree, Frank 48, 72
*Du Pree, Madame 48, 72
Dufemio, Antonio 42
Duffy, James T. 45
Dunbar, Agnes 71
Dunbar, J. O. 71, 91
*Duprez, Carl 63
Dutch Annie 82-83
Dyer, John 54-55
Earp, Allie 7-9, 12, 19
Earp, James 7-8, 13, 84
Earp, Mattie 19
Earp, Morgan 6, 8-13, 44, 84
Earp, Virgil 7-13, 23, 44, 66, 90
Earp, Wyatt 6-13,15-16,18, 66, 84, 90
Eastman, Charles 74
Eccleston, Mrs. 65
Eddy, George 46, 49

Edwards, Charles 45
Edwards, Mollie 68
Elliott, John 4
Elliott, M. A. 41
*Emerson, Mr. 63
Endlich, Jacob 52
Fallon, Mrs. S. E. 20, 69
Felter, Andrew J. 24
Fickas, Mrs. 69
Field, Edward 24, 52, 60-61
Fitzhenry, J. C. 72
Fly, Camillus 20
Fly, Mrs. C. S. (Mary "Mollie") 20
Fonck, Selma 78
*Foy, Lizzie 42
Friel, Christine 67
Fry, Henry 22
Fulkerson, Fannie 20
Fuller, Wesley 60
Fuzina, Richard 46
Garland, Frank 46, 49
Gaston, William Lee 13
Geisenhofer, O. W. 70
German, Joe 48
Ghilati, Catharine 21
Gillespie, John 5
Glover, Charles and Mrs. 67-68
Goldsmith, Richard 49
Goldsworthy, Richard 46
*Gonne, Mr. 43
Goodfellow, George Jr. 87
Goodfellow, George, M.D. 5, 6, 9, 55, 75, 87
*Gosper, Gov. John J. 28
*Grant, Ulysses S. 21
Gray, John Plesant 8,11-13, 60, 75
Gray, Mike 13, 24, 48, 52, 59-60
Gray, Smith 91
Gregory, J. H. 49
Gregory, Mrs. Carrie 50
Grounds, Billy 4-6, 52, 87
*Gutierez, Nodesto 63
Haggerty, Hugh 24

99

ILLUSTRATION CREDITS

Arizona State Library/Historical Society: Mollie Fly #94-0011, Tombstone City Band #97-2671

Author: Telegram, Wanted poster p. 56, Arizona Seal, saloon, Boothill photo, baseball player

Keith Davis: WANTED poster p. 14, Nellie Cashman, Golden Eagle Brewery, Tombstone City Cornet Band, Buckskin Frank Leslie, fighting roosters, gila monster, gamblers, Smith & Watson

Woodstockoperahouse.com: Patti Rosa

Worthpoint.com: Nellie Boyd

Kathy Franz has written three other books, all available on Amazon.com.

Forget Me Not: A Boothill Remembrance

Samuel Hammond Kettlewell: A Draughtsman's Remembrance

We Sent 'Em to Boothill

Made in the USA
Monee, IL
25 January 2024

52317753R00066